To Janie:

Wishing you
God's BEST!

Betty g Price

This is a gift of love
to you from Rachel.

101 WAYS TO FIX BROCCOLI

by

Betty J. Price

A Hearthstone Book

Carlton Press, Inc.   New York, N.Y.

The nutritional guides provided for each recipe are calculated based on the use of products listed in the Preface.

ISBN 0-8062-4707-X

Dedicated to

a precious mother, Miriam A. Sickles. Without her endless hours of assistance and encouragement this book could not have become a reality.

a great father, Grant E. Sickles, who provided the inspiration for the creation of this book with his request for "broccoli every day" when he was diagnosed with cancer.

a special husband, Harvey H. Price, who lovingly endured many months of taste-testing and will still eat broccoli. *His valuable constructive criticism helped ensure quality recipes.*

all the friends and relatives who assisted in taste-testing and offered numerous wonderful suggestions.

broccoli lovers throughout the world!

AUTHOR'S NOTE

100% of the profits received by the author from this book will be donated to designated ministries and charitable organizations.

CONTENTS

Vegetable Entrees

Broccoli & Meat
(or Meat Substitute) Dishes

FOREWORD

Broccoli is one of the healthiest foods on earth. It contains vitamins A, C, Beta carotene, fiber, and nitrogen compounds called indoles, which various studies indicate are effective in preventing cancer. Broccoli also contains significant amounts of calcium, potassium, thiamin, riboflavin, niacin, iron, and is low in sodium. A single cup of raw broccoli supplies your daily vitamin C and Beta carotene requirements, has less than ½ gram of fat and only 24 calories.

The word "broccoli" is derived from the Latin word *brachium*, which means branch or arm. This branch-like vegetable is a member of the cruciferous family, and has increased in popularity because of its anti-cancer properties. When sliced lengthwise, broccoli's inner stem portrays a cross-like pattern, thus the term cruciferous.

Every recipe (except Elephant Broccoli Stew, included just for fun) has been computer analyzed for specific nutrients. The simple format used makes it easy to track how much fat you're eating, both in grams and percent of total calories. Since it is known that excessive fat consumption is a major contributor to increasing your risk of heart disease, hypertension, diabetes, cancer, and obesity, this book can become a welcome addition to any health-conscious person's library.

According to government figures, per capita consumption of broccoli has increased 630 percent over the past twenty years. What better "welcoming mat" could there be for a cookbook on such a popular subject? Being health-minded can be enjoyable, and this book proves it.

Eating is one of life's greatest pleasures. The recipes in *101 Ways to Fix Broccoli* are so tasty that they dispel the myth If it tastes good it's either bad for you, or it's fattening.

Here is a cookbook that will offer easy, unique and tasty new ideas for those already incorporating a healthful diet in their lifestyle. And for those who are still exploring, *101 Ways to Fix Broccoli* could be the road toward a long and healthy life.

Barbara Kuntz Mallman, R.D.

Ms. Mallman is a member of the American Dietetic Association, Consulting Nutritionists of California, Heart Association Dining for Heart Committee, and Heart Association Speakers Bureau. She has served on a community nutrition task force, and been nutrition consultant for the San Diego Union.

PREFACE

Broccoli is receiving a lot of attention these days, and rightfully so, because of its high-density nutrient food value. It is considered one of the most nutritious vegetables. It is rich in vitamins (especially C) and protein, contains calcium, is low in fat and calories, has Beta carotene that is believed to reduce the risk of certain cancers, and is a good source of fiber.

SELECTION AND PREPARATION OF BROCCOLI

Choosing what to buy: Look for dark firm heads (smallest stalks) with tightly closed florets. Avoid yellowing and thick stems that may be overmature and could be tough and bitter. *Preparation*: Rinse head, cut off base of the stalk and remove leaves. Then decide how you are going to use the broccoli.

Spears—cut lengthwise into spears then cut a slash upward from the bottom about an inch to ensure even cooking.

Florets—cut florets from the stalk—*don't throw the stems away.* (If only florets are used, make another dish that uses chopped broccoli.)

Chopped—use the entire stalk along with any leftover stems. Chop through floret section, peel stems and slice lengthwise, then cut into ½″ cubes.

(RECIPES USING ONLY BROCCOLI STEMS)

Herbed Broccoli Salad	page 26	Teriyaki Broccoli	page 50
Gazpacho Broccoli Soup	page 44	Broccoli Muffins	page 97

Of course, you can use stems only for most recipes that specify chopped broccoli.

Equivalencies: (Approximates)

1 pound broccoli	= 2 stalks	1 cup grated cheese	= 4 oz.
1 stalk fresh broccoli, chopped	= 2½ cups	2 egg whites	= 1 egg
10 oz pkg of frozen broccoli*	= 2½ cups	3 Tbsp	= ¼ cup
16 oz pkg of frozen broccoli*	= 4 cups	4 Tbsp	= ⅓ cup

1 cup baking mix plus ¼ cup water = no cholesterol pie crust dough

Money-saving hint: Consider buying extra broccoli when it is on sale and make your own frozen chopped broccoli.

Abbreviations:

oz	= ounce	teas	= teaspoon	g	= grams	approx	= approximately
lb	= pound	Tbsp	= tablespoon	mg	= milligrams	pwd	= powdered
pkg	= package	opt	= optional	env	= envelope		

VEGETARIANS *please note*: Meat dishes have been included in this cookbook for those who prefer meat in their diet. Most of the recipes, however, are just as tasty *without the meat*. In fact, during the taste-testing process, family and friends frequently preferred them that way.

HEALTH-CONSCIOUS FOOD LOVERS

The recipes in this book list nutritional information, including calories, protein, carbohydrates, cholesterol, sodium, grams of fat, and percentage of calories from fat (all of the recipes *can* be prepared with 30% or less fat). The following products, which were available at the time of this writing, were used in calculating the values shown. New products are becoming available rapidly, so you are encouraged to check labels to determine the best options in your purchases.

baking mix	Jiffy—lower in fat, calories and sodium than other brands in my shopping area
cheese	Lifetime part skim milk (Cheddar, Swiss, Jack, Mozzarella)
chicken broth	Health Valley—fat-free "no salt" variety
chicken bouillon	Steero low-sodium powdered bouillon

corn muffin mix	Jiffy—it's lower in sodium, tastes good, and costs less!
cottage cheese	Knudsen Free (no sacrificing taste with this)
cream cheese	Philadelphia Light (better tasting than non-fat varieties currently available)
egg	Fleischmann's Egg Beaters or Healthy Choice Egg Substitute (whichever available)
frankfurters	Hebrew National Lite Beef Franks
ham	Swift Premium 96 percent fat-free smoked
margarine	Fleischmann's Extra Light corn oil spread
mayonnaise	Kraft Miracle Whip FREE (no fat, no cholesterol and it tastes good!)
milk	1 percent—various brands (our family taste preference rather than nonfat)
milk, evaporated	labels were checked for best buy on "light" skim milk varieties
mushrooms	Brandywine—it was the only brand I found that listed nutritional values
pickles, dill	kosher variety (they are lower in sodium)
salad dressing	labels checked for low-fat and sodium
salt	various salt substitutes such as Mrs. Dash, Accent, Spice Islands, No-Salt
snack crackers	low-salt varieties and "no fat" varieties when available—various brands
soups	Healthy Request: Vegetable, Cream of Chicken and Cream of Mushroom Campbell's dehydrated chicken noodle (lower in calories & sodium) Lipton dehydrated onion soup (lower in calories, fat & sodium) Lady Lee cream of celery (lower in fat and cost less too!)
sour cream	Knudsen Free
soy sauce	labels were checked for best buy in a low-sodium variety
tomato sauce	labels were checked for best buy in brands with "no salt added"

wheat germ   used instead of nuts to improve nutritional value without sacrificing taste

Learning to read labels grew into an interesting adventure. At first purchases were made solely on the basis of brands with the least amount of fat, but it didn't take long to learn that this may not always be the wisest choice. What a surprise it was to learn that frequently when fat is reduced, sodium is significantly increased. It was a special delight to find a nonfat product that was also tasty. On the other hand, when there was too much sacrifice of taste and/or texture with a nonfat product, a low-fat option was selected. Occasionally when all the brands had equal nutritional values with no sacrifice of flavor, a choice could be made based on the best price. It became fun to shop smarter and eat better!

NUTRITIONAL GUIDELINES:
It is rather meaningless to read labels on food products if you don't have any idea what you're checking for. A chart sharing appropriate amounts would have been included in this cookbook if that were possible, but there are too many variables, i.e., a person's age; gender; health; whether a person is trying to gain, lose or maintain weight, etc. A general rule of thumb is to keep cholesterol and saturated fat low, limit sodium intake, and try to keep calories from fats in your diet under 30 percent.

There are a number of organizations that provide helpful information at no charge:

American Cancer Society   American Heart Association
American Dietetic Association
U.S. Dept. of Health & Human Services—Nutrition Division

You can also check with your hospital or local chapter of the American Dietetic Association for advice from a Registered Dietitian.

SUBSTITUTION POSSIBILITIES:

FOOD	YOU CAN USE THESE INSTEAD
broccoli	*cruciferous vegetables such as cauli-flower, brussel sprouts, cabbage, kohlrabi*
2½ cups broccoli	*1 stalk; a 10-oz. package of frozen broccoli*
4 cups broccoli	*2 stalks; a 16-oz. bag of frozen broccoli*
all dairy products	*low-fat or nonfat varieties depending on your taste preference*
canned broth	*powdered flavored bouillon and water* (look for low sodium brands)
2 Tbsp flour	*1 Tbsp cornstarch for thickening*
1 clove garlic	*⅛ teas dry minced garlic OR ½ teas garlic juice*
1 cup diced chicken	*10 oz. can of chunk chicken (or turkey)*
sour cream	*1 cup cottage cheese whipped on high speed in a blender until smooth*
chopped nuts	*wheat germ—will decrease fat without sacrificing taste*

The use of tofu to stretch ground meat (use equal amounts of tofu and meat) and dairy products can increase the nutritive values as well as decrease fat, cholesterol and calories. If you prefer a meatless diet, you can buy products such as:

La Loma		*Worthington*	
Swiss Steak	Frankfurters	Country Stew	Meatballs
Fried Chicken	Tender Bits	Chili	Skallops
Nuteena	Vege-Burger	Steak	Choplets

There are many other options available and new products coming on the market all the time. It's refreshing to know that not only can you reap the benefits of a healthier body with good nutrition, you can also enjoy foods that taste good!

The preparation of this book opened up a new world to me. The challenge of creating was exciting. I now realize ways to fix broccoli may be limitless. I hope you'll not only enjoy the recipes in this cookbook, but will have some fun experimenting with your own creations.

Happy cooking!

ACKNOWLEDGMENTS

The nutritional values listed with the recipes in this cookbook could not have been included without the aid of some wonderful easy-to-use computer software that I purchased at a local computer store. One is *Health & Diet Pro* (© 1992, Digital Systems Research, Inc.). The nutritional components of over 3,000 foods included in this data base were developed by Barbara Kuntz Mallman, a Registered Dietitian now in private pratice, formerly the Head Dietitian at La Costa Spa and the Chief Nutritionist at Cardio-Fitness Centers in New York City. She is well-known through her lectures, interviews on television, and articles in major publications. Given the nominal cost of the program, I did not expect too much from it. What a pleasant surprise to find it tremendously valuable. By entering the ingredients for a proposed recipe, I was able to identify nutritional values, then make adjustments as needed, such as lowering fat or sodium. Then off I'd go to the kitchen for taste-testing to ensure that taste was not sacrificed for the sake of nutritional improvements.

The subsequent user-friendly software, which was recently featured on CNN, *Healthy Cooking Plus* (© 1992, Digital Systems Research, Inc.) is also very helpful as a tool for tracking and making nutritional adjustments. Menu plans allow a person to stay within nutritional guidelines. In just a matter of minutes you can complete a menu with individual portions automatically sized for the entire family. I highly recommend this software for use in every home!

It has been a real joy working with this software and Ms. Mallman.

101 WAYS TO FIX BROCCOLI

S
A
L
A
D
S

the only food that doesn't go up in price is food for thought

BROCCOLI SALAD BOWL

1 lb. broccoli florets
¼ cup French dressing
¼ cup chopped dill pickle
1 cup minced green pepper

2 Tbsp snipped parsley
1 Tbsp drained capers (opt)
1 hard boiled egg, diced

1. Prepare and steam broccoli until crispy tender (or prepare broccoli according to the package directions when using a purchased frozen product). Drain and set aside.
2. Combine dressing, pickle, green pepper, parsley and capers.
3. Stir the egg into the dressing mixture. Spoon mixture over the broccoli.
4. Cover and chill several hours or overnight.

Approx five servings
Per Serving*

Calories	65	*Cholesterol*	55 mg
Protein	6 g	*Sodium*	213 mg
Carbohydrates	11 g	*Fat*	1 g

Calories from fat = 16%
*Calculations based on use of products listed in the preface

BROCCOLI & CARROT L'ORANGE

2½ cups chopped broccoli
2 medium carrots, sliced
   diagonally

2 teas margarine
¼ cup frozen orange juice

1. Steam broccoli and carrots in lightly salted water until crispy tender.
2. Combine margarine and orange juice concentrate.
3. Heat just until the margarine melts.
4. Pour over vegetables and toss to coat. Chill before serving.

Approx three servings
Per Serving

Calories	78	Cholesterol	0 mg
Protein	6 g	Sodium	57 mg
Carbohydrates	15 g	Fat	1 g

Calories from fat = 15 %

PASTA BROCCOLI SALAD

Dressing
1 teas sesame oil
1½ teas vinegar
1 teas dried marjoram
1 clove minced garlic
¼ teas pepper

2½ cups broccoli florets
8 oz macaroni, cooked
1 sweet red pepper (½"
   strips)
1 small sweet onion, sliced
2 oz. cheese, cut in chunks
1 Tbsp chopped nuts

1. Combine all the dressing ingredients into a bowl. Whisk and set aside.
2. Prepare and steam broccoli until crispy tender (or prepare broccoli according to package directions when using a purchased frozen product). Drain.

3. Add dressing mixture to the broccoli.
4. Stir the broccoli mixture and cooked macaroni together.
5. Add red pepper, onion, cheese, and nuts. Toss well. Chill before serving.

Approx five servings
Per Serving

Calories	155	Cholesterol	4 mg
Protein	10 g	Sodium	43 mg
Carbohydrates	24 g	Fat	3 g

Calories from fat = 18%

PEANUT BROCCOLI SALAD

2 Tbsp mayonnaise
1 Tbsp Italian-type dressing
3 cups finely chopped
broccoli
¼ cup pickle relish

2 Tbsp minced onion
1 hard boiled egg, diced
salt and pepper to taste
1 oz chopped roasted peanuts

1. Thin mayonnaise with Italian dressing in a salad bowl.
2. Add remaining ingredients, except peanuts. Toss to coat with dressing.
3. Add the peanuts just before serving.

Approx four servings
Per Serving

Calories	155	Cholesterol	68 mg
Protein	8 g	Sodium	472 mg
Carbohydrates	24 g	Fat	5 g

Calories from fat = 29%

CONFETTI BROCCOLI SALAD

4 cups broccoli florets
3 grated carrots
1 diced red sweet pepper

½ avocado, diced
3–4 cups torn lettuce

1. Prepare and steam broccoli until crispy tender (or prepare broccoli according to package directions when using a purchased frozen product). Drain and cool.
2. Add remaining ingredients. Toss well. Serve with your favorite salad dressing.

Approx five servings
Per Serving

Calories	102	Cholesterol	0 mg
Protein	7 g	Sodium	54 mg
Carbohydrates	16 g	Fat	3 g

Calories from fat = 28%

HERBED BROCCOLI SALAD

2 teas canola cooking oil
2 Tbsp vinegar
⅛ teas garlic powder
½ teas salt; ⅛ teas pepper
other seasonings to taste
½ teas basil

3–4 broccoli stems
2 cups carrots, sliced
water (about 2″ in cooking pan)
2½ cups broccoli florets

1. Combine oil, vinegar, garlic powder, salt, pepper, and basil leaves in a bowl.
2. Finely slice the broccoli stems.
3. Place sliced broccoli stems and carrots in a saucepan with about 2″ water. Bring to a boil. Reduce heat and simmer about 2 minutes.
4. Add broccoli florets and simmer another minute. Drain vegetables.
5. Place vegetables in a bowl and toss with dressing.

6. Cover and chill until ready to serve.

Approx six servings
Per Serving

Calories	63	*Cholesterol*	0 mg
Protein	5 g	*Sodium*	36 mg
Carbohydrates	12 g	*Fat*	2 g

Calories from fat = 22%

BROCCOLI LINGUINE PRIMAVERA SALAD

2½ cups broccoli florets
8–12 oz linquine (pasta)
2 teas canola cooking oil
1 medium green pepper, cut
   in strips
1 small sweet red pepper,
   cut in strips
2 medium zucchini, grated

2 cloves minced garlic
1½ cups thinly sliced carrots
2 teas basil
1 teas oregano
½ teas salt
2 teas melted margarine
⅓ cup grated Parmesan
   cheese

1. Prepare and steam broccoli until crispy tender (or prepare broccoli according to package directions when using a purchased frozen product). Drain and set aside.
2. Cook linguine (you can substitute spaghetti or fettuccine) according to package directions. Drain and set aside.
3. Heat oil. Sauté the pepper strips until crispy tender. Add zucchini and garlic. Continue cooking for another minute.
4. Add carrots, broccoli, cooked pasta, seasonings, and margarine. Toss to coat.
5. Place in a serving dish. Top with Parmesan cheese. This is good hot or cold.

Approx eight servings
Per Serving

Calories	127	*Cholesterol*	3 mg
Protein	6 g	*Sodium*	103 mg
Carbohydrates	20 g	*Fat*	3 g

Calories from fat = 21%

MARINATED ITALIAN BROCCOLI SALAD MEDLEY

1¼ cup broccoli florets
1 cup cauliflower florets
2–3 tomatoes, cut in chunks
2–3 zucchini, sliced
1 Bermuda onion, thinly
  sliced

⅓ cup green pepper, chopped
⅓ cup stuffed green olives
½ cup Italian salad dressing

Combine all the ingredients in a large bowl. Refrigerate several hours, or overnight. Gently toss the salad just prior to serving.

Approx eight servings
Per Serving

Calories	38	Cholesterol	0 mg
Protein	2 g	Sodium	234 mg
Carbohydrates	7 g	Fat	1 g

Calories from fat = 21%

BROCCOLI POTATO SALAD

4 small red-skinned potatoes
2 teas margarine
½ teas salt
2½ cups broccoli florets
4 cups lettuce, torn in small
  pieces
1 cup finely shredded red
  cabbage
paprika to garnish

Dressing
2 Tbsp fresh lemon juice
¼ teas salt
2 Tbsp canola cooking oil
½ teas oregano
¼ teas basil
2 Tbsp salad dressing

1. Steam potatoes until almost tender, remove from heat and cut into ½″ cubes.
2. Melt margarine and pour over potatoes. Add salt and toss well.

3. Pre-heat broiler. Place potatoes on a cookie sheet and broil 5–10 minutes.
4. Prepare and steam broccoli until crispy tender (or prepare broccoli according to package directions when using a purchased frozen product). Drain.
5. Place lettuce, cabbage, and broccoli in a large bowl.
6. Put all the dressing ingredients in a bowl, and whip until smooth and creamy.
7. Pour dressing over salad. Top with potatoes and sprinkle with paprika.

Approx eight servings
Per Serving

Calories	120	Cholesterol	0 mg
Protein	4 g	Sodium	79 mg
Carbohydrates	21 g	Fat	3 g

Calories from fat = 24%

AVOCADO-BROCCOLI SALAD

3 cups chopped broccoli
¾ cup finely chopped celery
⅓ avocado, cut in chunks

1 head iceberg lettuce
½ cup cheese, cut in chunks
3 Tbsp Ranch dressing

Toss all the salad ingredients together and serve with your favorite meal.

Approx five servings
Per Serving

Calories	93	Cholesterol	2 mg
Protein	8 g	Sodium	154 mg
Carbohydrates	12 g	Fat	3 g

Calories from fat = 29%

BROCCOLI & CHEESE SALAD

2½ cups chopped broccoli
½ cup Cheddar cheese, cut in
    chunks
¼ cup minced onion
3 slices bacon fried crisp,
    crumbled
2 Tbsp sesame seeds (opt)

Dressing
¼ cup mayonnaise
1 Tbsp sugar
1½ teas vinegar

1. Mix the broccoli, cheese, onion, and bacon together. Set aside.
2. Blend dressing ingredients together. Pour over salad just prior to serving. Sprinkle sesame seeds (if desired) on top.

Approx five servings
Per Serving

Calories	120	*Cholesterol*	8 mg
Protein	10 g	*Sodium*	285 mg
Carbohydrates	14 g	*Fat*	4 g

Calories from fat = 28%

MANDARIN BROCCOLI TOFU SALAD

6 cups broccoli florets
¼ cup mayonnaise
¾ cup soft drained tofu
2 teas lemon juice
1 Tbsp honey

¼ cup raisins
¼ cup salted peanuts or
    cashews
1 can (11 oz) mandarin
    oranges
lettuce leaves

1. Prepare and steam broccoli until crispy tender (or prepare broccoli according to package directions when using a purchased frozen product). Drain and chill.
2. Put mayonnaise, tofu, lemon juice, and honey in blender. Blend until smooth and creamy. Chill until ready to serve.

3. Arrange broccoli and mandarin oranges on a bed of lettuce.
4. When ready to serve, add raisins and peanuts to dressing. Pour over salad.

Approx eight servings
Per Serving

Calories	122	Cholesterol	0 mg
Protein	7 g	Sodium	128 mg
Carbohydrates	23 g	Fat	2 g

Calories from fat = 18%

LAYERED BROCCOLI SALAD

2½ cups chopped broccoli
½ head iceberg lettuce
2 hard boiled eggs, diced
½ cup onion, chopped
1 cup frozen peas

1 cup mayonnaise
½ cup sour cream
½ cup grated cheese
5 slices crisply fried bacon

1. Prepare and steam broccoli until crispy tender (or prepare broccoli according to package directions when using a purchased frozen product). Drain.
2. Layer lettuce, eggs, onion, broccoli, and peas in a large glass dish.
3. Mix mayonnaise and sour cream together. Spread over the top layer.

NOTE—if you are watching sodium intake, consider replacing mayonnaise as follows:
   Mix ¼ cup mayonnaise, ¾ cup tofu and the sour cream together. Blend on high speed in a blender until smooth and creamy.

4. Sprinkle grated cheese and crumbled bacon on top of the salad.
5. Cover with plastic wrap and refrigerate about 24 hours before serving.

Approx six servings
Per Serving

Calories	210	*Cholesterol*	118 mg
Protein	15 g	*Sodium*	702 mg
Carbohydrates	27 g	*Fat*	6 g

Calories from fat = 26%

BROCCOLI-CELERY-RAISIN SALAD

4 cups finely chopped
  broccoli
½ cup finely chopped celery
½ cup raisins
¼ cup minced onion
chopped nuts (opt)

Dressing
½ cup mayonnaise
2 Tbsp sugar
1 Tbsp vinegar

1. Combine broccoli, celery, raisins, onion, and nuts (if desired). Mix together.
2. Blend dressing ingredients together. Pour over salad just prior to serving.

Approx six servings
Per Serving

Calories	105	*Cholesterol*	0 mg
Protein	5 g	*Sodium*	243 mg
Carbohydrates	26 g	*Fat*	less than ½ g

Calories from fat = 0% (about 8% with nuts)

ZUCCHINI-BROCCOLI MEDLEY

Marinade

1 Tbsp canola cooking oil
1 Tbsp fresh lemon juice
½ teas oregano
½ teas basil
½ teas salt; pepper to taste
1 clove minced garlic

2 teas margarine
½ cup minced onion
3 cups broccoli florets
2 cups zucchini, sliced
2 cups tomatoes, cut in chunks
8 oz macaroni, cooked
¼ cup red pepper, cut in thin strips

1. Whisk the marinade ingredients together until mixed well.
2. Melt margarine. Sauté onion until soft and transparent.
3. Combine onion, broccoli, zucchini, tomato, and marinade in a large bowl. Toss gently. Refrigerate several hours, or overnight.
4. Mix the broccoli mixture, cooked macaroni, and red pepper together. Garnish with parsley and/or pitted black olives if desired.

Approx eight servings
Per Serving

Calories	112	Cholesterol	0 mg
Protein	5 g	Sodium	26 mg
Carbohydrates	20 g	Fat	2 g

Calories from fat = 19%

BROCCOLI SALAD SUPREME

3 cups fresh broccoli florets
2 cups fresh cauliflower
   florets
1 cup celery, chopped
2–3 medium tomatoes,
   chopped

1 green pepper, chopped
⅓ cup stuffed green olives
½ cup cucumber salad
   dressing

1. Prepare vegetables. Place in a bowl and toss together.
2. Pour salad dressing over the vegetables.
3. Toss well and refrigerate until ready to serve.

Approx five servings
Per Serving

Calories	91	*Cholesterol*	0 mg
Protein	5 g	*Sodium*	343 mg
Carbohydrates	17 g	*Fat*	1 g

Calories from fat = 11%

S
O
U
P
S

*people don't care how much you know
until they know how much you care*

EASY BROCCOLI SOUP

1 pkg (16 oz) frozen chopped
  broccoli
1 Tbsp dried onion flakes
½ cup water

1 cup cream of chicken soup
1 cup milk
1 cup grated Cheddar cheese

1. Place broccoli (use about a pound of fresh broccoli if you
   prefer) and onion in a pan with the water. Simmer about 5
   minutes. *Do not drain.*
2. Add soup, milk and cheese. Continue cooking, stirring until
   heated through.

Approx four servings
Per Serving

Calories	147	*Cholesterol*	18 mg
Protein	18 g	*Sodium*	230 mg
Carbohydrates	13 g	*Fat*	4 g

Calories from fat = 25%

35

BROCCOLI SOUP ALMONDINE

⅓ cup blanched slivered
   almonds
1½ Tbsp margarine
1 cup onion, chopped
4 cups finely chopped
   broccoli
2 cups potato, cut in chunks

1 can (7 oz) chicken broth
1 cup water
½ teas basil
½ cup milk
¾ cup grated Cheddar
   cheese

1. Spread almonds in a single layer on a cookie sheet and bake at 350 degrees until lightly toasted (9–11 minutes). Let cool then finely grind.
2. Melt margarine over medium heat. Sauté onions until soft and lightly browned.
3. Stir in broccoli, potato, chicken broth, water, and basil. Cover and bring to a boil. Lower heat and simmer about 20 minutes until the potatoes are tender.
4. Remove from heat. Let cool slightly then purée in a food processor or blender.
5. Return soup to pan. Stir in milk, heating just to the boiling point.
6. Remove from heat. Fold in ½ cup cheese and the ground nuts (or wheat germ).
7. Ladle into soup bowls. Garnish with grated cheese.

Approx five servings
Per Serving
              Recipe as indicated

Calories	265	Cholesterol	6 mg
Protein	17 g	Sodium	287 mg
Carbohydrates	36 g	Fat	9 g

Calories from fat = 28%

Substituting wheat germ for the almonds

Calories	240	Cholesterol	6 mg
Protein	17 g	Sodium	286 mg
Carbohydrates	37 g	Fat	5 g

Calories from fat = 17%

CHICKEN BROCCOLI SOUP

3 cups milk
1 cup cream of chicken soup
½ cup grated cheese

2 ½ cups frozen chopped
   broccoli
1 cup frozen corn
1 cup diced cooked chicken

1. Mix milk and soup together.
2. Stir in cheese, broccoli, corn, and chicken.
3. Cook over medium heat, stirring occasionally, until heated through.

Approx five servings
Per Serving
        Recipe as indicated

Calories	272	*Cholesterol*	61 mg
Protein	29 g	*Sodium*	401 mg
Carbohydrates	25 g	*Fat*	8 g

Calories from fat = 25%

Without the chicken

Calories	223	*Cholesterol*	38 mg
Protein	21 g	*Sodium*	381 mg
Carbohydrates	25 g	*Fat*	6 g

Calories from fat = 23%

BEEF BROCCOLI SOUP

1 can (15 oz) tomatoes
1½ lbs. boneless chuck
2½ cups chopped broccoli
2 cups tomato juice
1 cup turnips, chopped
1 cup carrots, chopped

1 cup onion, chopped
1 cup celery, cut in chunks
2 cups cabbage, chopped
salt and pepper to taste
seasonings to taste

1. Drain tomatoes, but save juice.
2. Cut meat into 1½" size pieces and put with drained tomatoes in a large kettle. Pour water over meat until it is covered and cook slowly for one hour.
3. Add all the remaining ingredients and bring to a boil. Reduce heat and cook about 45 minutes longer until the vegetables are tender.

Approx eight servings
Per Serving
Recipe as indicated

Calories	223	Cholesterol	62 mg
Protein	30 g	Sodium	301 mg
Carbohydrates	14 g	Fat	6 g

Calories from fat = 25%

Without the beef

Calories	63	Cholesterol	0 mg
Protein	4 g	Sodium	246 mg
Carbohydrates	14 g	Fat	less than ½ g

Calories from fat = 7%

PASTA & BROCCOLI SOUP

2½ cups chopped broccoli
2 cups water
½ cups shell macaroni
½ small chopped onion
1 teas chicken flavor
   bouillon

2 tbsp flour
1 can (12 oz) evaporated milk
¾ cup grated Cheddar
   cheese

1. Combine water, broccoli, uncooked macaroni, onion, and chicken bouillon in a large saucepan. Bring to a boil.
2. Reduce heat and simmer until the macaroni is tender.
3. Combine flour and milk. Add it to the macaroni mixture. Cook over low heat until thickened.
4. Add cheese and continue cooking until cheese is melted.

Approx six servings
Per Serving

Calories	243	Cholesterol	11 mg
Protein	27 g	Sodium	215 mg
Carbohydrates	42 g	Fat	9 g

Calories from fat = 10%

AUSTRALIAN BROCCOLI SOUP

1 stalk broccoli, coarsely chopped
1 onion, chopped
1 acorn squash, peeled & chopped
2 teas chicken flavor bouillon

2 teas margarine
1 teas curry powder
other seasonings to taste
milk, to almost cover vegetables

1. Prepare broccoli, onion and squash (butternut is good too). Place in a saucepan.
2. Add chicken bouillon, curry powder, and other seasonings as desired.
3. Pour milk over vegetables until almost covered. Simmer until vegetables are soft.
4. Mash the vegetable mixture to make a thick soup.

Approx six servings
Per Serving

Calories	80	Cholesterol	1 mg
Protein	7 g	Sodium	50 mg
Carbohydrates	15 g	Fat	2 g

Calories from fat = 20%

BROCCOLI & CHEESE VEGETABLE SOUP

1 cup onion, chopped
2 Tbsp margarine
4 cups chopped broccoli
2 potatoes, diced
1 cup carrots, sliced
1 cup celery, chopped
3 cups water
⅓ cup sifted flour

6 teas chicken flavor
   bouillon
2 cups milk
salt, pepper, seasonings to
   taste
1½ cups grated Cheddar
   cheese

1. Melt margarine. Sauté onions until tender and transparent.
2. Combine vegetables and water in a saucepan. Bring to a
   boil then reduce heat and simmer about 30 minutes until
   vegetables are tender.
3. Combine flour, chicken flavor bouillon, and milk in a bowl.
   Beat until smooth.
4. Gradually blend into vegetable mixture and season to taste.
5. Add cheese and stir into soup until the cheese melts.

Approx six servings
Per Serving

Calories	240	*Cholesterol*	12 mg
Protein	20 g	*Sodium*	170 mg
Carbohydrates	33 g	*Fat*	6 g

Calories from fat = 20%

CREAM OF BROCCOLI SOUP

½ cup onion, chopped
1½ Tbsp margarine
¼ cup flour
2 cans (7 oz) chicken broth
4 cups chopped broccoli

1 cup celery, chopped
1 cup potato, cut in chunks
1 can (12 oz) evaporated milk
salt, pepper, seasonings to
   taste

1. Melt margarine. Sauté onions until soft and transparent.
2. Blend flour and chicken broth together.

3. Place broth, broccoli, celery and potato in a saucepan. Cook until vegetables are tender.
4. Remove from heat. Cool slightly then put soup mixture into a food processor or blender and purée. Return soup to pan.
5. Add milk and seasonings. Cook on medium heat until heated through.

Approx six servings
Per Serving

Calories	169	*Cholesterol*	3 mg
Protein	11 g	*Sodium*	131 mg
Carbohydrates	33 g	*Fat*	2 g

Calories from fat = 10%

BROCCOLI TUNA SOUP

1 cup water
1 teas chicken flavor
bouillon
2½ cups chopped broccoli
½ teas dried onion flakes
½ cup milk
¼ cup flour

½ cup grated Cheddar
cheese
1 can (6 oz) water-packed
albacore tuna, drained
⅓ cup almonds/lemon
wedges (opt)

1. Dissolve chicken bouillon in boiling water.
2. Add broccoli and onion to the chicken broth, and bring back to a boil.
3. Stir milk and flour together. Add to broccoli mixture. Cook until slightly thickened.
4. Fold in cheese, and continue cooking until cheese is melted.
5. Mix tuna (or, if you prefer, you can substitute canned salmon) into broccoli mixture and cook until heated through. Top with almonds (if desired).
6. Serve with lemon wedges (if desired) and your favorite crackers.

41

Approx four servings
Per Serving

Calories	160	*Cholesterol*	6 mg
Protein	22 g	*Sodium*	256 mg
Carbohydrates	16 g	*Fat*	3 g

Calories from fat = 15%

CURRIED BROCCOLI SOUP

4 cups chopped broccoli
1 large onion, chopped
1½ teas curry powder
 dash of garlic powder

1 can (7 oz) chicken broth
1 can (12 oz) evaporated milk
 salt & pepper to taste
¼ cup grated cheese

1. Place broccoli, onion, curry, garlic powder, and broth in a saucepan. Bring to a boil. Turn heat down and simmer for 4–5 minutes.
2. Place mixture in a blender and purée. Add milk and seasonings. Good hot or chilled.

Approx five servings
Per Serving

Calories	132	*Cholesterol*	5 mg
Protein	13 g	*Sodium*	129 mg
Carbohydrates	24 g	*Fat*	1 g

Calories from fat = 6%

RICE & BROCCOLI SOUP

1 can (7 oz) chicken broth
1 cup carrots, chopped
½ teas salt
⅛ teas pepper
other seasonings to taste

2½ cups chopped broccoli
¾ cup dry milk powder
¼ cup flour
1 ½ cups water
¾ cup quick-cook rice

1. Bring chicken broth, carrots, and desired seasonings to a boil. Lower heat. Simmer 5 minutes.
2. Add broccoli. Bring to boil then lower heat and simmer 5 more minutes until the vegetables are tender.
3. Combine milk powder, flour, and water. Add to the broccoli mixture.
4. Cook until thick and bubbly. Stir in rice, and remove from heat. Let stand about 5 minutes until the rice is tender.

Approx four servings
Per Serving

Calories	170	*Cholesterol*	3 mg
Protein	12 g	*Sodium*	103 mg
Carbohydrates	33 g	*Fat*	less than ½ g

Calories from fat = 1%

BROCCOLI & VEGGIES SOUP

4 cups chopped broccoli
2 potatoes, cut in chunks
1½ cups carrots, sliced
1 cup celery, chopped
2 cups cabbage, chopped
3–4 zucchini, cut in small pieces

1 cup turnips, chopped
other chopped vegetables as desired
1 packet dry onion soup mix
salt, pepper and seasonings to taste

1. Place all the ingredients into a large kettle.
2. Add enough water to cover the vegetables. Bring to a boil.
3. Reduce heat and simmer about 45 minutes until vegetables are tender.

Approx five servings
Per Serving

Calories	130	*Cholesterol*	0 mg
Protein	8 g	*Sodium*	210 mg
Carbohydrates	30 g	Fat	less than ½ g

Calories from fat = 2%

GAZPACHO BROCCOLI SOUP

1 can (24 oz) tomato juice
2 cups of tomatoes, crushed
1 can (15 oz) tomatoes with
  chilies
½ cup vinegar
⅓ cup sugar
¼ cup lemon juice
  salt and pepper to taste
  garlic powder to taste
2 Tbsp finely chopped
  parsley

2 broccoli stalks
2–3 celery stalks
½ cup onion
2 tomatoes
1 green pepper
1 zucchini
  jicama (opt)
1 cucumber (opt)
1 jar pimentos (opt)

This is best made at least a day before serving. It keeps well for several days in the refrigerator. It is nutritious as well as low in calories and can be served hot or cold.

1. Combine all the ingredients in the left column above in a soup tureen or a large glass bowl. Chill.
2. Peel the broccoli stalks, onion and cucumber (if desired). Finely chop the vegetables.
3. Add vegetables to the chilled sauce base, including jicama and pimentos (if desired) and serve with your favorite bread (warmed bread is really yummy) or crackers.

Approx eight servings
Per Serving

Calories	113	*Cholesterol*	0 mg
Protein	6 g	*Sodium*	284 mg
Carbohydrates	25 g	*Fat*	1 g

Calories from fat = 5%

44

E
N
T
R
E
E
S

a person can't think wrong and live right
anymore than they can plant weeds and harvest grain

PLAIN 'N' SIMPLE BROCCOLI

1–1½ pounds fresh broccoli   salt and pepper to taste

1. Clean and trim broccoli (you can save the stems to prepare other tasty dishes).
2. Steam until tender (about 10 minutes). Add seasonings to taste.
3. For variation, top with grated cheese or a cheese sauce.

Approx five servings
Per Serving

Calories	38	*Cholesterol*	0 mg
Protein	5 g	*Sodium*	28 mg
Carbohydrates	9 g	*Fat*	0 g

Calories from fat = 0%

45

STIR FRY BROCCOLI & VEGETABLES

1 teas canola oil
1 teas sesame seeds
¼ teas honey
1 lime, juiced
2 Tbsp low sodium soy sauce
  pepper to taste

2 stalks broccoli with stems
1 can (6 oz) water chestnuts
2 large shallots, thinly sliced
1 Tbsp safflower oil
2 cups cauliflower florets
1 carrot, cut diagonally

1. Heat oil in a skillet and toast sesame seeds until lightly browned (8–10 minutes). If desired, you can crush seeds on mortar with pestle or with a flat or heavy knife.
2. Stir honey, lime juice, soy sauce, and pepper into seeds. Set aside in a large bowl.
3. Remove florets from the broccoli. Cut stems in thin slices diagonally, rotating after each cut a quarter turn (this increases surface area for maximum absorption of seasonings). Set aside.
4. Heat wok or heavy skillet 1–2 minutes. Add oil and rotate pan to coat evenly.
5. Add shallots and stir fry for 2 minutes.
6. Add prepared broccoli stems, cauliflower, and carrot slices. Stir fry for 2–3 minutes.
7. Pour ⅓ cup water over the vegetables. Cover and steam until crispy tender.
8. Stir in broccoli florets and water chestnuts (add water). Steam until tender.
9. Continue to cook, uncovered, stirring constantly, until water has evaporated.
10. Pour some sesame seed mixture over the vegetables and toss to coat well.

Approx eight servings
Per Serving

Calories	83	Cholesterol	0 mg
Protein	6 g	Sodium	150 mg
Carbohydrates	14 g	Fat	2 g

Calories from fat = 26%

BROCCOLI IN MUSHROOM SAUCE

2½ cups chopped broccoli
1 can cream of mushroom
   soup

⅓ cup mayonnaise
1½ Tbsp sliced almonds

1. Preheat oven to 325 degrees.
2. Mix broccoli, soup, and mayonnaise together. Pour into a baking dish.
3. Top with sliced almonds to garnish. Bake 1 hour, or microwave 15–20 minutes.

Approx four servings
Per Serving

Calories	108	Cholesterol	6 mg
Protein	68 g	Sodium	537 mg
Carbohydrates	19 g	Fat	3 g

Calories from fat = 22%

BROCCOLI STUFFED TOMATOES

1 cup chopped broccoli
4 large ripe tomatoes
1 teas lemon juice
1 teas margarine
⅓ cup onion, chopped
⅓ cup milk
⅓ cup chicken broth

2 Tbsp flour
2 Tbsp grated Parmesan
   cheese
1 Tbsp fresh basil
1 egg white
   salt & pepper to taste

1. Pre-heat oven to 375 degrees.
2. Prepare and steam broccoli until crispy tender (or prepare broccoli according to package directions when using a purchased frozen product). Drain and set aside.
3. Remove tops from tomatoes and hollow, leaving about a ½" shell. Sprinkle with lemon juice and drain (save removed tomato for use in other recipes).
4. Melt margarine in a saucepan. Sauté onion until soft and transparent.

5. Whisk milk, chicken broth, and flour together. Add to onion and cook until sauce is thickened. Remove from heat. Stir in broccoli, cheese, and basil.
6. Beat egg white until stiff. Fold into broccoli mixture. Spoon into tomato shells.
7. Arrange filled tomatoes in a baking dish. Bake uncovered 30–35 minutes until puffed and lightly browned.

Approx four servings
Per Serving

Calories	100	Cholesterol	3 mg
Protein	6 g	Sodium	94 mg
Carbohydrates	16 g	Fat	2 g

Calories from fat = 17%

ALMONDINE BROCCOLI

1½ lbs. broccoli spears
1 can cream soup (your favorite)
½ cup liquid (milk or water)
½ teas salt, ¼ teas pepper

1 cup grated cheese
1½ cups bread crumbs
2 Tbsp margarine
¼ cup chopped almonds

1. Pre-heat oven to 300 degrees.
2. Lay broccoli in a baking dish then blend soup, liquid, salt and pepper together. Pour evenly over the broccoli. Spread grated cheese on top of the broccoli.
3. Melt margarine and add bread crumbs. Sprinkle over cheese. Top with almonds. Bake 45 minutes.

Approx eight servings
Per Serving

Calories	209	Cholesterol	9 mg
Protein	14 g	Sodium	369 mg
Carbohydrates	27 g	Fat	7 g

Calories from fat = 29%

BROCCOLI STRATA

4 cups chopped broccoli
1½ Tbsp margarine
1 onion, minced
⅓ cup flour
2 cups milk

¼ cup egg substitute
  (1 egg)
salt & pepper to taste
1 cup grated cheese
1 cup bread crumbs

1. Pre-heat oven to 350 degrees.
2. Prepare and steam broccoli until crispy tender (or prepare broccoli according to package directions when using a purchased frozen product). Drain and set aside.
3. Melt margarine and sauté onion in a saucepan. Blend flour, milk, egg, salt, pepper, and cheese together. Add to the onion. Cook until thickened.
4. Layer broccoli and sauce alternately. Top with bread crumbs. Bake about 30 minutes, or until lightly browned.

Approx five servings
Per Serving

Calories	269	*Cholesterol*	12 mg
Protein	20 g	*Sodium*	298 mg
Carbohydrates	38 g	*Fat*	6 g

Calories from fat = 21%

BROCCOLI WITH LEMON SAUCE

2 lbs. broccoli
2 Tbsp margarine
1 Tbsp flour
¼ cup egg substitute
  (1 egg)

juice of ½ lemon
2 Tbsp cream (opt)
½ teas salt
pepper to taste

1. Trim broccoli into spears with 2″–3″ of stem (save stems for other tasty dishes).
2. Put broccoli into salted boiling water and cook 5–7 minutes until crispy tender. Keep 1¼ cups of the cooking water.

Drain broccoli and put into serving dish.
3. Melt margarine in a small saucepan. Remove from heat. Stir in flour then gradually blend in the broccoli liquid. Bring to a boil. Simmer 10 minutes.
4. Remove sauce from heat. Mix eggs and lemon juice together. Blend into sauce. Add desired seasoning. Stir in cream (if desired) and pour sauce over broccoli.

Approx eight servings
Per Serving

Calories	67	Cholesterol	0 mg
Protein	7 g	Sodium	54 mg
Carbohydrates	12 g	Fat	1 g

Calories from fat = 20%

TERIYAKI BROCCOLI

3 cups broccoli stems (no florets)
2 teas canola cooking oil
1 clove minced garlic

1½ Tbsp low sodium soy sauce
¼ cup sesame seeds (opt)

1. Remove thick skin from broccoli stems. Slice thinly lengthwise.
2. Heat oil. Reduce heat and sauté garlic.
3. Add broccoli and cook 3–5 minutes until crispy tender.
4. Add soy sauce and toss. Sprinkle sesame seeds on top.

Approx five servings
Per Serving

Calories	49	Cholesterol	0 mg
Protein	5 g	Sodium	172 mg
Carbohydrates	8 g	Fat	1 g

Calories from fat = 25%

CORN & BROCCOLI MEDLEY

4 cups chopped broccoli
½ cup egg substitute
  (2 eggs)
1 cup milk
1 cup flour
½ teas salt; ⅛ teas pepper

other seasonings to taste
1 pkg (10 oz) frozen corn
½ cup onion, chopped
1 Tbsp melted margarine
1 cup grated cheese

1. Pre-heat oven to 325 degrees.
2. Prepare and steam broccoli until crispy tender (or prepare broccoli according to package directions when using a purchased frozen product). Drain and set aside.
3. Blend egg, milk, flour, and salt together.
4. Mix all the ingredients together. Pour into a baking pan. Bake 30–35 minutes.

Approx six servings
Per Serving

Calories	224	Cholesterol	8 mg
Protein	17 g	Sodium	110 mg
Carbohydrates	38 g	Fat	4 g

Calories from fat = 14%

BROCCOLI 'N' STUFFING

4 cups chopped broccoli
1 can cream of mushroom
  soup
1 Tbsp minced onion
¼ cup egg substitute
  (1 egg)

¾ cup grated cheese
 salt and pepper to taste
2 Tbsp margarine
2 cups herbed stuffing mix

1. Pre-heat oven to 350 degrees.
2. Prepare and steam broccoli until crispy tender (or prepare broccoli according to package directions when using a purchased frozen product). Drain and set aside.

3. Mix all the ingredients except margarine and 1 cup of the stuffing mix together.
4. Pour broccoli mixture into a baking dish. Top with remaining cup of stuffing mix. Dot with margarine (or melt and drizzle on top). Bake for 30 minutes.

Approx six servings
Per Serving

Calories	179	*Cholesterol*	6 mg
Protein	12 g	*Sodium*	505 mg
Carbohydrates	25 g	*Fat*	5 g

Calories from fat = 23%

PEPPERS & BROCCOLI

2 teas canola cooking oil
1 small onion, chopped
2 cloves minced garlic
1 Tbsp water

4 cups broccoli florets
1 small sweet red pepper (cut into thin strips)
1 teas oregano or basil

Heat oil in a skillet on medium for 1 minute. Add all the ingredients and cook 2 minutes. Cover skillet and reduce heat. Cook for 6–8 minutes, stirring frequently, until the vegetables are crispy tender.

Approx five servings
Per Serving

Calories	70	*Cholesterol*	0 mg
Protein	5 g	*Sodium*	28 mg
Carbohydrates	12 g	*Fat*	2 g

Calories from fat = 24%

BROCCOLI WITH BASIL

2 stalks fresh broccoli
1½ cups fresh basil
  (or parsley)
1 clove garlic
1 Tbsp nuts (your favorite)

1 Tbsp Parmesan cheese
⅓ cup chicken broth
2 teas lemon juice
seasonings to taste

1. Remove broccoli florets. Peel and thinly slice broccoli stems.
2. Put about 1″ of water in a large saucepan and bring to a boil. Add broccoli florets and stems. Cook until tender. Drain.
3. Put the remaining ingredients in a blender and blend about 20 seconds.
4. Pour over the cooked broccoli.

Approx four servings
Per Serving

Calories	90	*Cholesterol*	1 mg
Protein	9 g	*Sodium*	75 mg
Carbohydrates	16 g	*Fat*	2 g

Calories from fat = 16%

GOLDEN BROCCOLI

4 cups chopped broccoli
1 teas salt
 pepper to taste
2 teas lemon juice (opt)

1 can cream of mushroom
  soup
½ cup grated Cheddar
  cheese

1. Prepare and steam broccoli until crispy tender (or prepare broccoli according to package directions when using a purchased frozen product). Drain and set aside.
2. Add pepper, lemon juice, and soup (or, if you prefer, substitute *your favorite* cream soup, i.e., chicken, celery, etc.) and cook until heated through.

3. Pour into a baking dish. Top with cheese. Broil just until the cheese melts.

Approx five servings
Per Serving

Calories	91	*Cholesterol*	5 mg
Protein	9 g	*Sodium*	236 mg
Carbohydrates	13 g	*Fat*	2 g

Calories from fat = 17%

BROCCOLI & VEGETABLE HODGEPODGE

4 cups broccoli florets
2 cups zucchini, sliced
1 cup red pepper strips
2 Tbsp margarine
4 oz Cheddar cheese, cubed
1 Tbsp milk

1 cup noodles; cooked, drained
½ teas oregano
½ teas basil
salt and pepper to taste

1. Stir fry vegetables in the margarine. Reduce heat. Add cheese cubes. Continue cooking, stirring frequently, until the cheese melts.
2. Add remaining ingredients. Mix lightly and serve.

Approx six servings
Per Serving

Calories	147	*Cholesterol*	14 mg
Protein	13 g	*Sodium*	85 mg
Carbohydrates	18 g	*Fat*	5 g

Calories from fat = 28%

AU GRATIN BROCCOLI

4 cups chopped broccoli
1 can cream of mushroom soup
¾ cup grated cheese

½ cup milk
1 Tbsp low sodium soy sauce
½ cup wheat germ
1½ Tbsp melted margarine

1. Pre-heat oven to 375 degrees.
2. Prepare and steam broccoli until crispy tender (or prepare broccoli according to package directions when using a purchased frozen product). Drain and set aside.
3. Combine soup, cheese, milk, and soy sauce in a saucepan. Heat on low until the cheese melts. Mix in broccoli. Pour into a shallow baking dish.
4. Blend wheat germ and margarine together, and sprinkle topping on the broccoli. Bake 20–25 minutes until bubbly.

Approx six servings
Per Serving

Calories	144	Cholesterol	7 mg
Protein	14 g	Sodium	314 mg
Carbohydrates	16 g	Fat	5 g

Calories from fat = 29%

BROCCOLI PUFF

4 cups chopped broccoli
1 can cream of mushroom soup
½ cup grated cheese
¼ cup milk

¼ cup mayonnaise
¼ cup egg substitute (1 egg)
½ cup fine bread crumbs
1 Tbsp melted margarine

1. Pre-heat oven to 350 degrees.
2. Place broccoli into bottom of a baking dish. Stir soup and cheese together. Gradually blend in milk, mayonnaise, and egg. Pour over the broccoli.
3. Mix bread crumbs and margarine together. Sprinkle on top. Bake 45 minutes.

Approx six servings
Per Serving

Calories	131	Cholesterol	5 mg
Protein	10 g	Sodium	384 mg
Carbohydrates	19 g	Fat	3 g

Calories from fat = 20%

M
E
A
T

D
I
S
H
E
S

your actions speak so loud that I can't hear what you say

BROCCOLI LEFTOVER SURPRISE

1¼ cups chopped broccoli
⅓ cup onion, chopped
1 Tbsp margarine
½ cup (or more) leftover
  meat
½ cup (or more) leftover
  vegetables

1 Tbsp flour
1¾ cups milk
1 cup baking mix
¾ cup egg substitute
  (3 eggs)
⅔ cup grated cheese

1. Preheat oven to 325 degrees.
2. Prepare and steam broccoli until crispy tender (or prepare broccoli according to package directions when using a purchased frozen product). Drain and set aside.

3. Melt margarine in a saucepan then sauté meat and onion.
4. Stir in the vegetables and flour. Set aside to cool.
5. Put milk, baking mix, and eggs in a blender, and mix on high speed until smooth.
6. Mix half the cheese, the cooled meat/vegetables, and baking mix together.
7. Pour into a greased (preferably using a non-stick vegetable spray) baking dish.
8. Sprinkle remaining cheese on top and bake 45–50 minutes. Let set for a few minutes before cutting and serving.

Approx four servings
Per Serving

Recipe as indicated (averages of meats)

Calories	335	*Cholesterol*	37 mg
Protein	25 g	*Sodium*	417 mg
Carbohydrates	33 g	*Fat*	13 g

Calories from fat = 33%

Recipe with meat substitute

Calories	316	*Cholesterol*	10 mg
Protein	28 g	*Sodium*	494 mg
Carbohydrates	34 g	*Fat*	9 g

Calories from fat = 25%

Recipe with tofu

Calories	291	*Cholesterol*	10 mg
Protein	21 g	*Sodium*	403 mg
Carbohydrates	34 g	*Fat*	9 g

Calories from fat = 27%

Recipe without any meat

Calories	261	*Cholesterol*	10 mg
Protein	17 g	*Sodium*	398 mg
Carbohydrates	33 g	*Fat*	8 g

Calories from fat = 27%

RICE & PORK (OR CHICKEN) WITH BROCCOLI

3 cups water
1½ cups long grain white
rice
2 Tbsp low sodium soy sauce
2 Tbsp canola cooking oil
6 green onions, thinly sliced

4 cups chopped broccoli
2 cups thinly sliced celery
1 cup diced green pepper
1 can (6 oz) sliced water
chestnuts
1 cup finely chopped cooked
pork

1. Combine rice, water and soy sauce in a saucepan or a micro-wave safe bowl. Bring to a boil. Cover and reduce heat. Cook until water is absorbed and rice is tender.
2. Heat oil in a skillet. Add onions, broccoli, celery, pepper, water chestnuts, and mushrooms (if desired). Stir fry just until vegetables are crispy tender.
3. Add cooked rice and meat (pork, chicken, or use *your favorite* meat, or meat substitute). Continue stirring 3–4 minutes until heated through. If you prefer, mix only the meat and vegetables together and serve them over the rice.

Approx eight servings
Per Serving

Recipe with pork

Calories	319	Cholesterol	35 g
Protein	16 g	Sodium	203 mg
Carbohydrates	39 g	Fat	12 g

Calories from fat = 33%

Recipe with chicken

Calories	240	Cholesterol	15 mg
Protein	13 g	Sodium	187 mg
Carbohydrates	39 g	Fat	5 g

Calories from fat = 18%

Recipe with meat substitute

Calories	236	Cholesterol	0 mg
Protein	13 g	Sodium	222 mg
Carbohydrates	40 g	Fat	4 g

Calories from fat = 15%

Recipe without any meat

Calories	208	Cholesterol	0 mg
Protein	8 g	Sodium	175 mg
Carbohydrates	39 g	Fat	4 g

Calories from fat = 15%

CHICKEN (OR TURKEY) BROCCOLI PUFF

4 cups chopped broccoli
2 Tbsp margarine
3 Tbsp flour
1 cup milk
1 teas lemon juice
¼ teas paprika
1 teas salt
dash of pepper

other seasonings to taste
1 cup diced cooked chicken/
  turkey
½ cup egg substitute
  (2 eggs)
4 egg whites
1 cup baking mix
¼ cup water

1. Pre-heat oven to 375 degrees.
2. Prepare and steam broccoli until crispy tender (or prepare broccoli according to package directions when using a purchased frozen product). Drain and set aside.
3. Melt margarine. Blend in flour. Gradually add milk, stirring constantly over low heat until thick and smooth.
4. Combine sauce, broccoli, lemon juice, paprika, salt, pepper, and diced meat.
5. Blend eggs into creamed mixture. Cool slightly.
6. Beat egg whites until stiff. Fold into the broccoli and meat mixture.
7. Blend baking mix and water to form dough. Roll out and fit into a pie plate. Place the broccoli mixture in the pastry shell and bake 40 minutes.

Approx eight servings
Per Serving

Recipe with chicken

Calories	220	Cholesterol	16 mg
Protein	14 g	Sodium	339 mg
Carbohydrates	29 g	Fat	6 g

Calories from fat = 25%

Recipe with turkey

Calories	218	Cholesterol	15 mg
Protein	14 g	Sodium	339 mg
Carbohydrates	29 g	Fat	6 g

Calories from fat = 24%

Recipe with meat substitute

Calories	216	Cholesterol	1 mg
Protein	14 g	Sodium	375 mg
Carbohydrates	30 g	Fat	5 g

Calories from fat = 22%

Recipe without any meat

Calories	188	Cholesterol	1 mg
Protein	9 g	Sodium	327 mg
Carbohydrates	29 g	Fat	5 g

Calories from fat = 23%

CHICKEN (OR TURKEY) BROCCOLI CREPES

1 lb. finely chopped broccoli
1 cup diced cooked chicken/
   turkey
1 can cream of chicken soup
⅓ cup onion, chopped
¼ cup grated Parmesan
   cheese
1 cup milk
⅓ cup sliced toasted almonds
   (opt)

Crepes
¼ cup egg substitute
   (1 egg)
1 cup milk
1 Tbsp canola oil
1 cup flour
Blend together
Make thin pancakes

1. Pre-heat oven to 350 degrees.
2. Prepare and steam broccoli until crispy tender (or prepare broccoli according to package directions when using a purchased frozen product). Drain and set aside.
3. Mix chicken (or turkey), broccoli, half of the soup (if you prefer, you can use cream of mushroom soup instead of chicken), onion, and cheese together.
4. Spoon heaping tablespoons of filling into each crepe. Roll and place seam side down in a baking dish. (This makes about a dozen crepes.)
5. Blend the remaining soup with the milk and pour the sauce over the crepes.
6. Sprinkle crepes with almonds (if desired). Bake 30 minutes.

Approx eight servings
Per Serving

Recipe with chicken

Calories	177	*Cholesterol*	20 mg
Protein	13 g	*Sodium*	239 mg
Carbohydrates	23 g	*Fat*	5 g

Calories from fat = 25%

Recipe with turkey

Calories	176	*Cholesterol*	19 mg
Protein	14 g	*Sodium*	239 mg
Carbohydrates	23 g	*Fat*	5 g

Calories from fat = 24%

Recipe with meat substitute

Calories	173	Cholesterol	6 mg
Protein	14 g	Sodium	274 mg
Carbohydrates	24 g	Fat	4 g

Calories from fat = 23%

Recipe without any meat

Calories	146	Cholesterol	6 mg
Protein	9 g	Sodium	227 mg
Carbohydrates	23 g	Fat	4 g

Calories from fat = 24%

CASHEW CHICKEN (OR TURKEY) BROCCOLI CREPES

2½ cups finely chopped broccoli
1 cup diced cooked chicken/ turkey
2 cups finely chopped celery
2 Tbsp minced onion
1 pkg (10 oz) frozen peas
½ cup mayonnaise
2 Tbsp low sodium soy sauce
⅓ cup cashews, coarsely chopped

½ cup green pepper (opt)
chopped pimento (opt)
dozen crepes (see recipe previous page)
1½ Tbsp margarine
2 Tbsp flour
salt and pepper to taste
1 cup milk
¾ cup grated Cheddar cheese

1. Pre-heat oven to 350 degrees (you can micro-cook rather than bake this dish if you prefer).
2. Prepare and steam broccoli until crispy tender (or prepare broccoli according to package directions when using a purchased frozen product). Drain and set aside.
3. Mix chicken (or turkey), broccoli, celery, onion, peas, mayonnaise, soy sauce, cashews, and optional ingredients (if desired), together in a large bowl.
4. Spoon heaping tablespoons of filling into each crepe and

roll, placing seam side down in baking dish. (See recipe for crepes on the previous page.)

5. Melt margarine. Blend in flour, salt, a dash of pepper, and the milk.
6. Cook mixture until slightly thickened. Add cheese and cook just until melted.
7. Pour cheese sauce over the crepes. Sprinkle with paprika for garnish, if desired. Micro-cook for 20 minutes on 70 percent power or bake 45 minutes.

Approx six servings
Per Serving

Recipe with chicken

Calories	357	Cholesterol	27 mg
Protein	26 g	Sodium	566 mg
Carbohydrates	43 g	Fat	12 g

Calories from fat = 30%

Recipe with turkey

Calories	355	Cholesterol	26 mg
Protein	26 g	Sodium	566 mg
Carbohydrates	43 g	Fat	12 g

Calories from fat = 29%

Recipe with meat substitute

Calories	352	Cholesterol	8 mg
Protein	26 g	Sodium	613 mg
Carbohydrates	44 g	Fat	11 g

Calories from fat = 28%

Recipe without any meat

Calories	315	Cholesterol	8 mg
Protein	19 g	Sodium	549 mg
Carbohydrates	43 g	Fat	10 g

Calories from fat = 29%

MICROWAVE CHICKEN (OR TURKEY) BROCCOLI BURRITOS

5 cups finely chopped broccoli
½ cup grated sharp cheese
1 cup diced cooked chicken/turkey
1 can cream of celery soup
1 can (4 oz) diced green chilies

¼ cup chopped green onion (opt)
1 dozen small flour tortillas
1 can cream of mushroom soup
½ cup grated Cheddar cheese
½ cup sliced ripe olives (opt)

1. Prepare and steam broccoli until crispy tender (or prepare broccoli according to package directions when using a purchased frozen product). Drain.
2. Combine broccoli, cheese, chicken (or turkey), celery soup, chilies, and onion.
3. Spoon filling down the center of tortillas, and roll up jellyroll fashion. Place seam down in a microwave-safe baking dish.
4. Spread mushroom soup evenly over tortillas. Top with cheese and olives.
5. Micro-cook on high 5 minutes, or until the cheese melts.

Approx eight servings
Per Serving

Recipe with chicken

Calories	275	Cholesterol	18 mg
Protein	15 g	Sodium	662 mg
Carbohydrates	37 g	Fat	8 g

Calories from fat = 25%

Recipe with turkey

Calories	274	Cholesterol	16 mg
Protein	15 g	Sodium	662 mg
Carbohydrates	37 g	Fat	7 g

Calories from fat = 24%

Recipe with meat substitute

Calories	271	*Cholesterol*	3 mg
Protein	15 g	*Sodium*	698 mg
Carbohydrates	38 g	*Fat*	7 g

Calories from fat = 23%

Recipe without any meat

Calories	244	*Cholesterol*	3 mg
Protein	10 g	*Sodium*	650 mg
Carbohydrates	37 g	*Fat*	6 g

Calories from fat = 24%

CHICKEN (OR TURKEY) BROCCOLI DELIGHT

1½ lbs. frozen broccoli spears
2 cups diced cooked chicken/ turkey
1 can cream of celery soup
1 can cream of chicken soup

⅓ cup mayonnaise
2 Tbsp lemon juice
¼ teas curry powder (opt)
⅔ cup grated Cheddar cheese

1. Pre-heat oven to 350 degrees.
2. Cook broccoli according to package directions. Drain and place in the bottom of a greased (preferably with a non-stick vegetable spray) baking dish.
3. Place chicken (or turkey) over broccoli.
4. Mix remaining ingredients, except cheese, together and pour evenly over meat.
5. Sprinkle cheese on top and bake 25 minutes.

Approx eight servings
Per Serving

Recipe with chicken

Calories	182	*Cholesterol*	35 mg
Protein	18 g	*Sodium*	533 mg
Carbohydrates	15 g	*Fat*	6 g

Calories from fat = 29%

Recipe with turkey

Calories	180	Cholesterol	33 mg
Protein	19 g	Sodium	553 mg
Carbohydrates	15 g	Fat	6 g

Calories from fat = 28%

Recipe with meat substitute

Calories	175	Cholesterol	6 mg
Protein	19 g	Sodium	623 mg
Carbohydrates	17 g	Fat	5 g

Calories from fat = 24%

Recipe without any meat

Calories	120	Cholesterol	6 mg
Protein	8 g	Sodium	528 mg
Carbohydrates	15 g	Fat	4 g

Calories from fat = 28%

CHICKEN (OR TURKEY) BROCCOLI PIE

2½ cups chopped broccoli
⅓ cup onion, chopped
1 small green pepper,
    chopped
1 cup diced cooked chicken/
    turkey
¾ cup baking mix

1½ cups milk
¾ cup egg substitute
    (3 eggs)
salt and pepper to taste
other seasonings to taste
¾ cup grated cheese

1. Pre-heat oven to 375 degrees.
2. Prepare and steam broccoli until crispy tender (or prepare broccoli according to package directions when using a purchased frozen product). Drain and set aside.
3. Mix chicken (turkey), broccoli, onion, and pepper together in a baking dish.

4. Combine baking mix, milk, egg, and seasoning in a blender. Blend until smooth.
5. Pour over broccoli and meat. Sprinkle cheese on top. Bake 35–40 minutes.

Approx six servings
Per Serving

Recipe with chicken

Calories	249	Cholesterol	26 mg
Protein	20 g	Sodium	358 mg
Carbohydrates	28 g	Fat	7 g

Calories from fat = 24%

Recipe with turkey

Calories	247	Cholesterol	25 mg
Protein	20 g	Sodium	358 mg
Carbohydrates	28 g	Fat	6 g

Calories from fat = 23%

Recipe with meat substitute

Calories	244	Cholesterol	7 mg
Protein	20 g	Sodium	405 mg
Carbohydrates	29 g	Fat	6 g

Calories from fat = 22%

Recipe without any meat

Calories	207	Cholesterol	7 mg
Protein	13 g	Sodium	342 mg
Carbohydrates	28 g	Fat	5 g

Calories from fat = 23%

BROCCOLI CHICKEN (OR TURKEY) & RICE QUICHE

2 cups cooked rice
½ cup grated cheese
¼ cup egg substitute
  (1 egg)
½ teas salt
4 cups finely chopped
  broccoli
½ cup chopped onion
1 cup diced cooked chicken/
  turkey

¾ cup egg substitute
  (3 eggs)
1 can (5 oz) evaporated milk
  seasonings to taste
1 can (4 oz) sliced
  mushrooms
¾ cup grated Cheddar
  cheese

1. Combine rice, cheese, egg and salt. Press firmly into a pie plate.
2. Steam broccoli. Mix in onion and chicken (or turkey). For a tasty variation, you can use ½–¾ cup low-fat grated Mozzarella cheese instead of meat.
3. Mix eggs, milk, seasoning and mushrooms together. Add chicken (or cheese).
4. Blend broccoli and egg mixtures together. Spoon into the rice shell.
5. Sprinkle cheese on top. Microwave 10–12 minutes.

Approx six servings
Per Serving

Recipe with chicken

Calories	261	Cholesterol	29 mg
Protein	27 g	Sodium	249 mg
Carbohydrates	34 g	Fat	4 g

Calories from fat = 14%

Recipe with turkey

Calories	259	Cholesterol	27 mg
Protein	27 g	Sodium	249 mg
Carbohydrates	34 g	Fat	4 g

Calories from fat = 13%

Recipe with Mozzarella cheese

Calories	256	Cholesterol	10 mg
Protein	27 g	Sodium	296 mg
Carbohydrates	35 g	Fat	3 g

Calories from fat = 11%

Recipe without any meat

Calories	219	Cholesterol	10 mg
Protein	20 g	Sodium	232 mg
Carbohydrates	34 g	Fat	3 g

Calories from fat = 10%

CHICKEN & BROCCOLI

1 lb. fresh broccoli
1 clove minced garlic
6 chicken breast filets
  (halves)
½ teas salt

pepper to taste
1 cup sour cream
1 pkg onion soup mix
2 egg whites, stiffly beaten
¼ cup Parmesan cheese

1. Pre-heat oven to 350 degrees.
2. Prepare and steam broccoli until crispy tender. Drain. Place in a baking dish.
3. Brown chicken breasts with garlic and other seasonings to taste (preferably in a non-stick pan or using a non-stick vegetable spray) until brown on both sides.
4. Cook over low heat until tender. Remove from heat. Cool then cut in chunks.
5. Combine sour cream, onion soup and pan juices. Spread half the mixture over the broccoli. Top with chicken chunks.
6. Fold egg whites into the remaining sour cream mixture. Spread over chicken.
7. Sprinkle with Parmesan cheese and bake 20 minutes, or until nicely browned.

Approx six servings
Per Serving

Calories	241	*Cholesterol*	77 mg
Protein	36 g	*Sodium*	317 mg
Carbohydrates	13 g	*Fat*	5 g

Calories from fat = 20%

BROCCOLI CHEESE CHICKEN

2½ cups broccoli florets   ½ cup water or milk
4 half chicken breasts   ⅛ teas pepper
1 can cheese soup   other seasonings to taste

1. Prepare and steam broccoli until crispy tender (or prepare broccoli according to package directions when using a purchased frozen product). Drain and set aside.
2. Cook chicken (preferably in a non-stick pan or using a non-stick vegetable spray) until brown on both sides—about ten minutes.
3. Stir in soup, water, and pepper. Heat until the mixture comes to a boil.
4. Reduce heat. Add broccoli. Cover and simmer 10 minutes, stirring occasionally, until chicken and broccoli are tender.

Approx four servings
Per Serving

Calories	218	*Cholesterol*	76 mg
Protein	35 g	*Sodium*	295 mg
Carbohydrates	11 g	*Fat*	4 g

Calories from fat = 17%

MONTE CARLO BROCCOLI CHICKEN

4 cups chopped broccoli
3 chicken breasts (cut in
  half)
1 can cream of chicken soup
1 Tbsp lemon juice

½ cup mayonnaise
¾ teas curry powder
other seasonings to taste
⅔ cup grated sharp cheese

1. Pre-heat oven to 350 degrees. (This is even better made the day before serving it.)
2. Prepare and steam broccoli until crispy tender (or prepare broccoli according to package directions when using a purchased frozen product). Drain. Place in the bottom of a baking dish. Lay chicken over the broccoli.
3. Combine soup, lemon juice, mayonnaise, and curry powder. Pour over chicken.
4. Sprinkle cheese on top. Bake 30–45 minutes, or until the chicken tests done.

Approx six servings
Per Serving

Calories	252	Cholesterol	81 mg
Protein	36 g	Sodium	528 mg
Carbohydrates	17 g	Fat	5 g

Calories from fat = 18%

BROCCOLI SHEPHERD'S PIE

1 lb. broccoli, chopped
1 Tbsp margarine
1 clove garlic
1 lb. stew meat
1 lb. carrots, cut in chunks
3 potatoes, cut in chunks
1 can (15 oz) stewed
  tomatoes

1 pkg dry onion soup mix
1 can cream of
  mushroom soup
1½ cups water
seasonings to taste

1. Preheat oven to 300 degrees.
2. Prepare and steam broccoli until crispy tender (or prepare broccoli according to package directions when using a purchased frozen product). Drain and set aside.
3. Cut meat into cubes. Melt margarine. Sauté garlic and stew meat.
4. Combine all of the ingredients into a baking dish and cover with water. Bake 4 hours. To thicken: whisk 3 Tbsp flour in ⅔ cup water. Fold through stew. Serve with biscuits or dinner rolls.

Approx six servings
Per Serving

Recipe as indicated

Calories	310	Cholesterol	55 mg
Protein	24 g	Sodium	471 mg
Carbohydrates	33 g	Fat	11 g

Calories from fat = 30%

Without the beef

Calories	163	Cholesterol	1 mg
Protein	7 g	Sodium	443 mg
Carbohydrates	33 g	Fat	2 g

Calories from fat = 7%

BROCCOLI BEEF SQUARES

4 cups chopped broccoli
1 lb. lean ground beef
1¼ cups grated cheese
½ cup onion, chopped
½ cup water
2 cups baking mix

½ cup milk
¼ cup grated Parmesan
cheese
1 teas salt
dash pepper

1. Pre-heat oven to 375 degrees.
2. Prepare and steam broccoli until crispy tender (or prepare broccoli according to package directions when using a purchased frozen product). Drain and set aside.
3. Brown beef in skillet. Drain off fat.
4. Stir in ¾ cup of the grated cheese and the chopped onion.
5. Blend water, baking mix, and remaining ½ cup grated cheese together to form a soft dough. Pat in a dish, pressing about ½" up the sides.
6. Sprinkle half the meat mixture over the dough.
7. Spread broccoli evenly over the meat.
8. Top with the remaining meat.
9. Mix remaining ingredients together. Pour over the top layer of meat.
10. Bake 25–30 minutes. Cut in squares to serve.

Approx eight servings
Per Serving

Recipe as indicated

Calories	435	Cholesterol	46 mg
Protein	26 g	Sodium	641 mg
Carbohydrates	46 g	Fat	17 g

Calories from fat = 35%

Without the meat

Calories	320	Cholesterol	9 mg
Protein	16 g	Sodium	609 mg
Carbohydrates	46 g	Fat	9 g

Calories from fat = 25%

GROUND BEEF & BROCCOLI

1 lb. chopped broccoli
1 lb. lean ground beef
1 medium onion, chopped
2 cloves minced garlic
1 Tbsp margarine
3 Tbsp flour

1 cup water
1 can (15 oz) tomatoes
2 Tbsp catsup
½ teas salt
⅛ teas pepper
seasonings to taste

1. Pre-heat oven to 350 degrees.
2. Prepare and steam broccoli until crispy tender (or prepare broccoli according to package directions when using a purchased frozen product). Drain and set aside.
3. Place beef, onion, and garlic in a skillet. Cook until browned.
4. Spoon meat into a baking dish. Spread broccoli evenly over the meat.
5. Melt margarine. Blend in flour. Add water and cook until bubbly.
6. Stir in tomatoes, catsup and desired seasoning. Simmer for about 5 minutes.
7. Pour sauce mixture over broccoli. Cover and bake 30 minutes.

Approx six servings
Per Serving

Recipe as indicated

Calories	241	Cholesterol	49 mg
Protein	19 g	Sodium	259 mg
Carbohydrates	18 g	Fat	12 g

Calories from fat = 45%

With meat substitute

Calories	142	Cholesterol	0 mg
Protein	16 g	Sodium	310 mg
Carbohydrates	19 g	Fat	2 g

Calories from fat = 15%

BROCCOLI MEATLOAF SUPREME

1 lb. chopped broccoli
1 lb. lean ground beef
½ cup onion, chopped
½ cup celery, chopped
½ green pepper, chopped
1½ cups dry bread crumbs
1 can (8 oz) tomato sauce

1 teas salt
1 clove minced garlic
other seasonings to taste
½ cup egg substitute
  (2 eggs)
½ cup grated cheese

1. Pre-heat oven to 350 degrees. *Delicious option: use wheat germ instead of ground beef.*
2. Prepare and steam broccoli until crispy tender (or prepare broccoli according to package directions when using a purchased frozen product). Drain.
3. Blend all the ingredients together, and mold into a loaf shape.
4. Bake for one hour. (You might want to bake potatoes at the same time).

Approx six servings
Per Serving

Recipe as indicated

Calories	325	*Cholesterol*	54 mg
Protein	26 g	*Sodium*	298 mg
Carbohydrates	29 g	*Fat*	13 g

Calories from fat = 35%

Substituting wheat germ for ground beef

Calories	238	*Cholesterol*	4 mg
Protein	18 g	*Sodium*	255 mg
Carbohydrates	40 g	*Fat*	4 g

Calories from fat = 16%

SICILIAN BROCCOLI STROMBOLI

1¼ cups chopped broccoli
½ lb. lean ground meat
½ cup onion, chopped
1 can (15 oz) Italian style
tomatoes
¼ teas pepper
½ teas Italian seasoning
sesame or poppy seeds

½ cup green pepper, chopped
¼ cup sliced ripe olives
½ cup sliced mushrooms
(optional)
1 cup grated Mozzarella
cheese
milk (as needed)
1 pkg (10 oz) pizza dough

1. Pre-heat oven to 375 degrees.
2. Prepare and steam broccoli until crispy tender (or prepare broccoli according to package directions when using a purchased frozen product). Drain and set aside.
3. Cook meat and onion until meat is no longer pink and the onion is tender. Drain fat off.
4. Stir in broccoli, tomatoes (undrained), pepper, and Italian seasoning. Bring to a boil. Reduce heat and simmer uncovered until the liquid nearly evaporates.
5. Add green pepper, olives, and mushrooms. Cool while preparing dough.
6. Roll pizza dough out. Cut dough into four triangles. Spoon ¼ of the meat mixture down the center of each piece of dough.
7. Sprinkle with cheese.
8. Moisten edges of dough with milk, and draw the long edges together over the filling, stretching and pinching together to seal. Arrange seam side down on a baking dish.
9. Prick tops with a fork and brush with milk.
10. Sprinkle with sesame or poppy seeds. Bake 25–30 minutes or until lightly browned.

Approx eight servings
Per Serving

Recipe as indicated

Calories	288	*Cholesterol*	29 mg
Protein	20 g	*Sodium*	547 mg
Carbohydrates	32 g	*Fat*	10 g

Calories from fat = 32%

Calories	209	Cholesterol	4 mg
Protein	13 g	Sodium	525 mg
Carbohydrates	32 g	Fat	5 g

Calories from fat = 20%

HAM & BROCCOLI

4 cups chopped broccoli
1 cup cooked ham, cubed
1 can cream of celery soup
3/4 cup grated Swiss cheese

8 oz cooked noodles
1/2 teas dry mustard (opt)
3/4 cup milk
1 can French Fried onions

1. Pre-heat oven to 350 degrees.
2. Prepare and steam broccoli until crispy tender (or prepare broccoli according to package directions when using a purchased frozen product). Drain and set aside.
3. Combine all the ingredients, except the French fried onions, in a baking dish.
4. Cut through onions with a knife. Top broccoli and ham mixture with the onions. Bake about 20 minutes until heated through.

Approx six servings
Per Serving

Calories	264	Cholesterol	33 mg
Protein	15 g	Sodium	486 mg
Carbohydrates	35 g	Fat	9 g

Calories from fat = 30%

HAM STEAKS WITH SWEET POTATOES & BROCCOLI

2½ cups chopped broccoli
1 teas margarine
1 teas grated lemon rind
½ cup water
1 Tbsp flour
1 can (7 oz) chicken broth

1 teas dry mustard (opt)
¼ teas ground ginger
2 teas lemon juice
1 can (29 oz) sweet potatoes
2 teas margarine
1 lb. fully cooked ham steak

1. Put broccoli, water, margarine, and lemon rind in saucepan. Cover and bring to a full boil. Reduce heat and cook 6–8 minutes, or until tender.
2. Blend flour and chicken broth. Whisk in mustard, ginger, and lemon juice.
3. Cook until slightly thickened. Add sweet potatoes and heat through.
4. Melt margarine. Cook ham until heated through. Cut in four pieces.

Approx four servings
Per Serving
Calories	199	*Cholesterol*	26 mg
Protein	10 g	*Sodium*	321 mg
Carbohydrates	38 g	*Fat*	6 g

Calories from fat = 21%

79

C
A
S
S
E
R
O
L
E
S

When you share a sorrow you cut it in half;
when you share a joy you double it!

QUICK 'N' EASY BROCCOLI & RICE CASSEROLE

4 servings quick-cook rice
1 can cream of mushroom
   soup

8 oz chunked cheese
1½ lbs. chopped broccoli,
   cooked

1. Pre-heat oven to 350 degrees. (micro-cook rather than bake this dish if you prefer).
2. Cook rice according to package directions.
3. Heat soup and cheese until cheese melts. Add rice. Pour over broccoli. Place in a baking dish. Bake about 20 minutes (microwave on high about 10 minutes).

Approx six servings
Per Serving

Calories	278	Cholesterol	13 mg
Protein	22 g	Sodium	267 mg
Carbohydrates	41 g	Fat	4 g

Calories from fat = 14%

CAULIFLOWER-BROCCOLI STRATA

2½ cups broccoli florets
1½ cups cauliflower florets
6 slices French bread
¾ cup sharp Cheddar cheese
1 cup milk
1 cup egg substitute
  (4 eggs)

¼ cup sliced green onions
¼ teas salt
⅛ teas dry mustard (opt)
⅛ teas pepper
6 thin slices of tomato
1½ teas Parmesan cheese

1. Pre-heat oven to 350 degrees.
2. Clean and trim broccoli and cauliflower. Steam over boiling water until crispy tender. Drain and set aside.
3. Cut bread into ½" cubes and arrange evenly in a greased baking dish.
4. Top with ½ cup of the grated cheese then the broccoli and cauliflower.
5. Combine milk, eggs, onion, salt, mustard (optional), and pepper. Stir well. Pour over the vegetables. Cover with foil and chill for one hour.
6. Cut ten 1" slits in foil and bake for 1¼ hours, or until liquid is absorbed.
7. Uncover. Top with tomato slices and remaining Cheddar cheese. Sprinkle Parmesan cheese on top and return to the oven just until the cheese melts.

Approx six servings
Per Serving

Calories	198	Cholesterol	6 mg
Protein	15 g	Sodium	310 mg
Carbohydrates	28 g	Fat	3 g

Calories from fat = 14%

VERSATILE BROCCOLI VEGGIE BAKE

4 cups broccoli florets
1 pkg (10 oz) frozen
    cauliflower
1 pkg (10 oz) frozen corn
1 can (15 oz) cream corn
2 cups grated cheese
½ teas salt

1 cup cottage cheese
1 pkg (14 oz) tofu
1 can cream of celery soup
1 can (4 oz) sliced
    mushrooms
1½ cups soft bread crumbs
½ Tbsp melted margarine

1. Preheat oven to 375 degrees.
2. Prepare and steam broccoli until crispy tender (or prepare broccoli according to package directions when using a purchased frozen product). Drain and set aside.
3. Mix cauliflower, corn, grated cheese and salt together.
4. Put cottage cheese, tofu, and soup in a blender, and blend until smooth.
5. Fold broccoli, soup mixture, and mushrooms into vegetables. Pour into a baking dish.
6. Toss bread crumbs with margarine until evenly coated. Sprinkle on casserole.
7. Bake 30–35 minutes. Allow standing time of 10 minutes before serving.

Approx ten servings
Per Serving

Calories	95	*Cholesterol*	68 mg
Protein	8 g	*Sodium*	314 mg
Carbohydrates	14 g	*Fat*	2 g

Calories from fat = 26%

Recipe without the tofu

Calories	241	*Cholesterol*	8 mg
Protein	19 g	*Sodium*	441 mg
Carbohydrates	33 g	*Fat*	6 g

Calories from fat = 20%

Recipe with ground beef

Calories	335	Cholesterol	45 mg
Protein	27 g	Sodium	471 mg
Carbohydrates	32 g	Fat	13 g

Calories from fat = 34%

Recipe with meat substitute · ·

Calories	264	Cholesterol	8 mg
Protein	25 g	Sodium	514 mg
Carbohydrates	33 g	Fat	6 g

Calories from fat = 19%

Recipe with diced cooked chicken

Calories	270	Cholesterol	31 mg
Protein	24 g	Sodium	458 mg
Carbohydrates	32 g	Fat	7 g

Calories from fat = 22%

BROCCOLI RATATOUILLE GARDEN PIE

1½ Tbsp margarine
1–2 cloves garlic, minced
⅓ cup onion, chopped
1 cup finely chopped broccoli
½ cup green pepper, chopped
1 cup eggplant, chopped
1 cup zucchini, chopped
½ cup tomato, chopped
salt to taste

⅛ teas pepper
½ teas basil
1¼ cup milk
¼ teas sour cream (opt)
1 can (8 oz) tomato sauce
¾ cup egg substitute
  (3 eggs)
¾ cup baking mix
1 cup grated cheese

1. Preheat oven to 375 degrees, and lightly grease a large baking dish (preferably with a non-stick vegetable spray).
2. Melt margarine in a large pan. Sauté garlic, onion, broccoli, green pepper, eggplant, zucchini, and tomato until vegetables are crispy tender.

3. Mix in all the remaining ingredients, except the cheese. Pour into a baking dish.
4. Sprinkle cheese evenly over the top. Bake 35–40 minutes until a knife or toothpick inserted near the center comes out clean.

Approx eight servings
Per Serving

Calories	172	Cholesterol	5 mg
Protein	9 g	Sodium	202 mg
Carbohydrates	23 g	Fat	5 g

Calories from fat = 26%

VEGGIE BROCCOLI CASSEROLE

1 Tbsp margarine
1 small onion, chopped
1 lb. chopped broccoli
2 tomatoes, chopped
1 cup celery, chopped
1 green pepper, chopped
salt & pepper to taste

other seasoning to taste
½ cup diced Swiss cheese
½ cup diced Cheddar cheese
1 cup dry bread crumbs
½ cup grated Cheddar cheese

1. Pre-heat oven to 350 degrees.
2. Melt margarine. Sauté onions until tender and transparent.
3. Add diced cheese. Reduce heat. Add vegetables and steam until crispy tender.
4. Spoon into a baking dish. Top with bread crumbs and grated cheese. Bake 30 minutes.

Approx six servings
Per Serving

Calories	188	Cholesterol	8 mg
Protein	15 g	Sodium	219 mg
Carbohydrates	25 g	Fat	4 g

Calories from fat = 22%

CORN & BROCCOLI CASSEROLE

2½ cups chopped broccoli
1 pkg (10 oz) frozen corn
1 teas dry onion flakes
½ cup grated cheese

2 Tbsp milk
¼ cup crushed snack
    crackers

1. Cook broccoli, corn, and onion flakes until broccoli is almost tender. Drain.
2. Stir in cheese and milk. Spoon into a baking dish. Bake until the cheese is melted and the broccoli is tender.
3. Sprinkle crushed crackers on top and serve.

Approx four servings
Per Serving

Calories	155	*Cholesterol*	5 mg
Protein	12 g	*Sodium*	137 mg
Carbohydrates	27 g	*Fat*	3 g

Calories from fat = 16%

BROCCOLI MUSHROOM CASSEROLE

4 cups chopped broccoli
½ cup egg substitute
    (2 eggs)
1 can cream of mushroom
    soup (or your favorite)

1 cup mayonnaise
1 cup grated cheese
1 teas chopped onion
1 cup crushed Cheez-it
    crackers

1. Pre-heat oven to 350 degrees.
2. Prepare and steam broccoli until crispy tender (or prepare broccoli according to package directions when using a purchased frozen product). Drain and set aside.
3. Mix remaining ingredients, except the crackers, together. Stir in the broccoli.
4. Top with crushed crackers and bake 45 minutes.

Approx six servings
Per Serving

Calories	180	*Cholesterol*	7 mg
Protein	12 g	*Sodium*	726 mg
Carbohydrates	26 g	*Fat*	5 g

Calories from fat = 25%

LAYERED RICE & BROCCOLI CASSEROLE

2½ cups broccoli florets
2 zucchini, sliced
⅓ cup green pepper
2 Tbsp green onion
1 large tomato, sliced
2 cups cooked rice

1 cup diced cooked chicken
1 cup grated cheese
1 cup sour cream
1 can (4 oz) diced
green chilies
seasonings to taste

1. Preheat oven to 350 degrees.
2. Steam broccoli and zucchini. Chop green pepper and onion. Slice the tomato.
3. Layer in a baking dish: rice, chicken, 1 cup cheese, broccoli, zucchini, tomato.
4. Mix the remaining ingredients together and pour over the broccoli mixture.
5. Sprinkle the reserved cheese over the top. Bake 30 minutes.

Approx six servings
Per Serving

Recipe as indicated

Calories	205	*Cholesterol*	25 mg
Protein	20 g	*Sodium*	98 mg
Carbohydrates	25 g	*Fat*	4 g

Calories from fat = 18%

Without the meat

Calories	163	*Cholesterol*	6 mg
Protein	13 g	*Sodium*	82 mg
Carbohydrates	25 g	*Fat*	2 g

Calories from fat = 14%

MAKE-AHEAD HAMBURGER/BROCCOLI CASSEROLE

1 lb. finely chopped broccoli
1 cup carrots, sliced
1 lb. lean ground beef
⅓ cup onion, chopped
1 clove minced garlic
1 can (32 oz) tomato sauce

salt & pepper to taste
1 cup sour cream
1 cup cottage cheese
8 oz noodles, cooked, drained
1 cup grated Cheddar cheese
parsley for garnish (opt)

1. Pre-heat oven to 350 degrees.
2. Steam broccoli and carrots until crispy tender. Drain and set aside.
3. Brown beef with chopped onion and garlic. Drain off fat. Stir in tomato sauce, salt and pepper. Simmer, uncovered, for 5 minutes.
4. Combine sour cream, cottage cheese, broccoli, carrots, and noodles.
5. Place the noodle mixture into a baking dish. Spoon meat mixture on top.
6. Sprinkle with cheese and bake for 30 minutes, or put in the refrigerator and bake later (add a little more baking time). Garnish with parsley.

Approx eight servings
Per Serving

Recipe as indicated

Calories	301	Cholesterol	60 mg
Protein	26 g	Sodium	151 mg
Carbohydrates	29 g	Fat	10 g

Calories from fat = 30%

Without the meat

Calories	186	Cholesterol	23 mg
Protein	15 g	Sodium	118 mg
Carbohydrates	29 g	Fat	2 g

Calories from fat = 10%

HAM & BROCCOLI CASSEROLE

2½ cups chopped broccoli
1 cup cooked ham, cubed
¾ cup grated cheese
½ cup baking mix

1½ cups milk
½ cup egg substitute
(2 eggs)

1. Pre-heat oven to 350 degrees.
2. Prepare and steam broccoli until crispy tender (or prepare broccoli according to package directions when using a purchased frozen product). Drain.
3. Spread into an ungreased baking dish. Layer ham and cheese over the broccoli.
4. Beat remaining ingredients together until smooth. Pour evenly over the cheese.
5. Bake uncovered for one hour.

Approx five servings
Per Serving

Calories	199	Cholesterol	11 mg
Protein	16 g	Sodium	363 mg
Carbohydrates	25 g	Fat	5 g

Calories from fat = 24%

CREOLE BROCCOLI FRANKS

2 teas margarine
1 clove minced garlic
⅓ cup onion, chopped
4 cups finely chopped
    broccoli
½ green pepper, chopped
½ cup celery, chopped
½ cup tomato juice

1½ Tbsp cornstarch
½ teas salt
¼ teas sugar
⅛ teas basil
other seasonings to taste
4 frankfurters, sliced
4 servings quick-cook rice
½ cup grated cheese

1. Melt margarine. Sauté garlic, onion, broccoli, green pepper, and celery until tender.

89

2. Add ¾ cup of the tomato juice to the broccoli and frankfurt-ers. Mix well.
3. Cook over medium heat, stirring frequently. Simmer while preparing rice.
4. Prepare instant rice according to package instructions.
5. Combine the remaining ¼ cup tomato juice with cornstarch, salt, sugar and basil. Add to the broccoli/franks mixture. Cook over medium heat until thick and bubbly.
6. Spoon vegetables and franks over cooked rice. Sprinkle cheese on top.

Approx six servings
Per Serving

Calories	263	*Cholesterol*	20 mg
Protein	14 g	*Sodium*	371 mg
Carbohydrates	36 g	*Fat*	8 g

Calories from fat = 28%

CORNY TUNA BROCCOLI CASSEROLE

1 Tbsp margarine
¼ cup onion, chopped
1 can (6½ oz) chunk light tuna (use the water packed variety)
1 red or green pepper, chopped
1 pkg (8 oz) Jiffy corn muffin mix

¼ cup egg substitute (1 egg)
½ cup milk
seasoning to taste, or leave plain
2½ cups finely chopped broccoli
1 cup sour cream
1 cup grated Cheddar cheese

1. Pre-heat oven to 375 degrees.
2. Melt margarine and sauté onions. Add tuna and pepper. Heat through.
3. Combine corn muffin mix, egg, milk and desired seasonings. Stir until moist, but still lumpy. Add broccoli and tuna mix-ture. Spoon into a baking dish.

4. Spread sour cream evenly over broccoli mixture. Sprinkle cheese on top. Bake for 35–40 minutes. If desired, garnish with sprigs of parsley.

Approx six servings
Per Serving

Calories	298	*Cholesterol*	7 mg
Protein	21 g	*Sodium*	507 mg
Carbohydrates	38 g	*Fat*	7 g

Calories from fat = 21%

QUICK TUNA DIVAN

2 pkg (10 oz) frozen broccoli spears
1 can (10 oz) vegetable soup
¼ cup milk

1 can (7 oz) water packed tuna (drained and flaked)
2 Tbsp grated Parmesan cheese

1. Cook broccoli according to package directions. Drain and set aside.
2. Heat soup and milk, stirring until well blended.
3. Arrange broccoli in a shallow broiler-proof baking dish.
4. Top with tuna. Pour sauce over tuna, and sprinkle cheese on top.
5. Slide under broiler, about 4" from heat, and cook until bubbly.

Approx four servings
Per Serving

Calories	180	*Cholesterol*	3 mg
Protein	19 g	*Sodium*	591 mg
Carbohydrates	21 g	*Fat*	2 g

Calories from fat = 12%

CRAB & BROCCOLI PUFF

1 lb. chopped broccoli
1 pkg dry onion soup mix
1 egg, separated

1 can (14 oz) crab meat
1 teas lemon juice
¼ cup mayonnaise

1. Prepare and steam broccoli until crispy tender (or prepare broccoli according to package directions when using a purchased frozen product). Drain and set aside.
2. Drain crab meat then flake, add lemon juice and set aside.
3. Prepare onion soup following package directions. Slowly beat the egg yolk into the soup. Then fold in the crab.
4. Beat egg white until soft peaks form. Fold in mayonnaise.
5. Spoon crab mixture over the broccoli and top with the egg white mixture.
6. Broil 4″ away from heat about 5 minutes, or until puffy and golden brown. Serve immediately.

Approx five servings
Per Serving

Calories	95	*Cholesterol*	82 mg
Protein	11 g	*Sodium*	563 mg
Carbohydrates	12 g	*Fat*	2 g

Calories from fat = 16%

BROCCOLI SUPREME

1 lb. chopped broccoli
3 cups cottage cheese
¾ cup egg substitute
  (3 eggs)
3 Tbsp margarine
⅓ cup flour
⅓ cup onion, chopped

1 pkg (10 oz) frozen corn
6 oz Cheddar cheese, cubed
½ teas salt
⅛ teas pepper
other seasonings to taste
1 cup soft bread crumbs

1. Pre-heat oven to 350 degrees.
2. Prepare and steam broccoli until crispy tender (or prepare

broccoli according to package directions when using a purchased frozen product). Drain and set aside.
3. Blend cottage cheese, eggs, 1 Tbsp margarine, and flour together until smooth.
4. Fold in onions, corn, cheese, broccoli, and seasoning. Pour into a baking dish.
5. Sauté bread crumbs in remaining 2 Tbsp margarine and sprinkle over broccoli mixture. Bake for 1 hour.

Approx six servings
Per Serving

Calories	337	*Cholesterol*	10 mg
Protein	28 g	*Sodium*	470 mg
Carbohydrates	45 g	*Fat*	7 g

Calories from fat = 19%

STUFFING MIX & BROCCOLI CASSEROLE

2½ cups chopped broccoli
1 cup egg substitute
(4 eggs)
1½ cups milk

2 cups chicken flavor
stuffing mix
1¼ cups grated cheese
⅛ teas nutmeg

1. Pre-heat oven to 375 degrees.
2. Prepare and steam broccoli until crispy tender (or prepare broccoli according to package directions when using a purchased frozen product). Drain and set aside.
3. Combine eggs and milk. Stir in stuffing mix, ¾ cup cheese, broccoli and the nutmeg. Pour into a baking dish.
4. Sprinkle with remaining cheese and bake 45 minutes.

Approx four servings
Per Serving

Calories	278	*Cholesterol*	15 mg
Protein	26 g	*Sodium*	677 mg
Carbohydrates	33 g	*Fat*	6 g

Calories from fat = 18%

93

BROCCOLI & HERB STUFFING MEDLEY

4 cups chopped broccoli
3½ Tbsp melted margarine
4 Tbsp flour
2 teas pwd chicken bouillon
1 cup milk

1½ cups water
2 cups herb stuffing mix
⅓ cup celery, chopped
⅓ cup pecans (optional)

1. Pre-heat oven to 350 degrees.
2. Prepare and steam broccoli until crispy tender (or prepare broccoli according to package directions when using a purchased frozen product). Drain and set aside.
3. Melt 2 Tbsp margarine. Add flour, the powdered chicken bouillon and milk.
4. Mix the broccoli and sauce together. Pour into a casserole dish.
5. Combine stuffing mix, water, remaining 1½ Tbsp margarine, celery and nuts.
6. Spread evenly over broccoli and bake 25 minutes. (Can be made a day ahead.)

Approx six servings
Per Serving

Calories	177	Cholesterol	2 mg
Protein	8 g	Sodium	356 mg
Carbohydrates	30 g	Fat	5 g

Calories from fat = 24%

MEXICAN BROCCOLI MEDLEY

1½ lbs. chopped broccoli
3 cups cooked rice
1¼ cups grated cheese
1 cup sour cream
1 green pepper, chopped

1 can diced green chilies
1 teas oregano
1 clove minced garlic
seasonings to taste

1. Preheat oven to 350 degrees.
2. Prepare and steam broccoli until crispy tender (or prepare broccoli according to package directions when using a purchased frozen product). Drain.
3. Grease a large casserole dish (preferably with a non-stick vegetable spray). Layer ingredients as follows: rice, ¾ cup of the cheese, and broccoli.
4. Mix sour cream, green pepper, chilies, oregano, garlic, and onion together.
5. Add salt, pepper, other desired seasoning to taste. Pour over broccoli mixture.
6. Sprinkle the remaining cheese on top. Bake 30 minutes.

Approx eight servings
Per Serving

Calories	167	*Cholesterol*	5 mg
Protein	14 g	*Sodium*	82 mg
Carbohydrates	27 g	*Fat*	2 g

Calories from fat = 12%

CURRIED BROCCOLI & RICE CASSEROLE

4 cups broccoli
2 cups quick-cook rice
1 Tbsp dry minced onion
  flakes
½ cup egg substitute
  (2 eggs)

1 cup grated cheese
½ cup milk
1 teas curry powder (or basil,
  if you prefer)
other seasonings to taste

1. Pre-heat oven to 350 degrees.
2. Cut broccoli lengthwise into spears, then steam and drain.
3. Cook rice with dried onion according to package directions.
4. Stir eggs, ½ cup of the cheese, milk and spices together. Add to the rice.
5. Pour into a baking dish and arrange broccoli on top. Sprinkle with remaining cheese and bake about 20 minutes, or until set.

Approx five servings
Per Serving

Calories	183	Cholesterol	8 mg
Protein	16 g	Sodium	168 mg
Carbohydrates	27 g	Fat	3 g

Calories from fat = 13%

P
O
T
P
O
U
R
R
I

a smile increases your face value

BROCCOLI MUFFINS

3–4 broccoli stems
1 cup whole wheat flour*
1 cup all purpose flour
½ cup wheat germ
1 Tbsp baking powder
½ teas baking soda
1 teas cinnamon
¼ teas each: allspice,
   nutmeg

¼ cup egg substitute
   (1 egg)
⅔ cup firmly packed brown
   sugar
1 cup buttermilk
¼ cup canola oil 2 Tbps 2 Tblspn
1 teas vanilla flavoring applesauce
½ cup raisins

1. Preheat oven to 350 degrees.
2. Peel broccoli stems. Grate about one cup. Set aside.
3. Combine flours, wheat germ, baking powder, baking soda,
   and seasonings into a medium-size bowl.

*for a lighter muffin replace the wheat flour with all purpose flour

4. In a large bowl stir together egg, brown sugar, buttermilk, oil, and vanilla.
5. Stir broccoli and raisins into moist mixture.
6. Add flour to broccoli mixture. Gently fold together until dry ingredients are moistened.
7. Fill muffin cups (about ¾ full for medium size) and bake 20–25 minutes or until a toothpick inserted in the center comes out clean.

This is a versatile recipe because it is so easily adaptable. You might want to experiment with some of the following:

♦ add ½ cup of your favorite nuts (use nuts instead of wheat germ)
♦ eliminate the raisins—substitute your favorite fruit
♦ use grated cheese instead of seasonings, flavoring and raisins
♦ make into a loaf cake instead of muffins and serve with whip topping
♦ be as creative as you like

On occasion when I want *some of the pleasure without too much guilt*, I'll substitute chocolate chips for the raisins . . . *mmmmmm good!*

Makes one dozen large muffins (18 medium size)
Per Serving

Calories	~~167~~ 123	*Cholesterol*	1 mg
Protein	5 g	*Sodium*	34 mg
Carbohydrates	37 g	*Fat*	2 ~~4~~ 9 g

Calories from fat = ~~18~~ 9%

BROCCOLI CORNBREAD

2½ cups finely chopped
   broccoli
¼ cup melted margarine
¼ cup egg substitute
   (1 egg)
½ cup finely chopped onion
1 cup small curd cottage
   cheese

1 green pepper, chopped
   (opt)
½ cup grated Cheddar
   cheese
1 box (8 oz) Jiffy cornbread
   mix

1. Preheat oven to 375 degrees.
2. Prepare and steam broccoli until crispy tender (or prepare broccoli according to package directions when using a purchased frozen product). Drain.
3. Add all the remaining ingredients, except the cornbread mix.
4. Fold in cornbread mix and pour into a baking dish. Bake 40 minutes, or until browned.

Approx eight servings
Per Serving

Calories	193	*Cholesterol*	2 mg
Protein	10 g	*Sodium*	317 mg
Carbohydrates	27 g	*Fat*	6 g

Calories from fat = 27%

PITA BROCCOLI/VEGETABLE SANDWICH

1 cup finely chopped broccoli
2 grated carrots
3 Tbsp finely grated red
   cabbage
1½ Tbsp mayonnaise

salt, seasonings to taste
½ cup shredded lettuce
½ cup alfalfa sprouts (opt)
4 slices avocado (opt)
2 teas sesame seeds (opt)
2 pocket pita bread

1. Mix broccoli, carrot, cabbage, mayonnaise, and desired seasonings together.

2. Cut each of the pita breads in half and spoon broccoli mixture into pita.
3. Top with remaining ingredients.

Approx four servings
Per Serving

Calories	122	*Cholesterol*	0 mg
Protein	5 g	*Sodium*	273 mg
Carbohydrates	25 g	*Fat* less than	½ g

Calories from fat = 3%

BROCCOLI LASAGNA

4 cups chopped broccoli
1 Tbsp margarine
½ cup onion, chopped
1 clove minced garlic
1 can (15 oz) tomato sauce
1 pkg spaghetti seasoning
¼ cup egg substitute (1 egg)

½ cup grated Parmesan cheese
2 cups cottage cheese
seasonings to taste
1 cup grated Mozarella cheese
8 oz lasagna noodles, cooked

(This Recipe works great with finely chopped stems only)

1. Preheat oven to 350 degrees.
2. Prepare and steam broccoli until crispy tender (or prepare broccoli according to package directions when using a purchased frozen product). Drain and set aside.
3. Melt margarine in a saucepan. Sauté onion and garlic. Add tomato sauce and spaghetti seasoning. Bring to a boil. Reduce heat and simmer about 20 minutes.
4. Combine egg, grated Parmesan cheese, cottage cheese, and desired seasonings in a blender. Blend on high speed until smooth.
5. Layer in a large baking dish:

Bottom Layer: ⅓ of the sauce, ⅓ the noodles, ½ the cheese mixture, ½ the broccoli, ½ the Mozzarella cheese.

Second Layer: another ⅓ sauce and ⅓ noodles, the remaining cheese mixture and the rest of the broccoli.

Top Layer: remaining ⅓ noodles and ⅓ sauce, topped with the rest of the Mozzarella cheese.

6. Bake 40 minutes. For a tasty treat, serve with warm garlic bread.

Approx eight servings
Per Serving

Calories	167	Cholesterol	8 mg
Protein	17 g	Sodium	331 mg
Carbohydrates	19 g	Fat	4 g

Calories from fat = 19%

STUFFED GREEN PEPPER DELIGHT

1¼ cups chopped broccoli
1 cup cooked rice
⅓ cup onion, chopped
¼ cup celery, chopped
1 cup dry bread crumbs
1 can (8 oz) tomato sauce
1 clove minced garlic

1 teas salt
other seasoning to taste
½ cup egg substitute
    (2 eggs)
½ cup grated cheese
4–6 green peppers

1. Pre-heat oven to 350 degrees.
2. Prepare and steam broccoli until crispy tender (or prepare broccoli according to package directions when using a purchased frozen product). Drain.
3. Blend all the ingredients, except the peppers, together in a large bowl.
4. Remove stems and seeds from the peppers (cut in half if you prefer).
5. Fill peppers with the broccoli mixture. Top with catsup or parsley for garnish.

6. Bake for 35 minutes, or until the peppers test done.

Approx four servings
Per Serving

Calories	240	*Cholesterol*	6 mg
Protein	13 g	*Sodium*	262 mg
Carbohydrates	41 g	*Fat*	3 g

Calories from fat = 10%

EASY BROCCOLI PIE

1 Tbsp margarine
2½ cups chopped broccoli
1 small onion, chopped
1 clove minced garlic
¼ cup mushrooms (opt)
½ teas Italian seasoning
¼ teas ginger (opt)
salt & pepper to taste

other seasoning to taste
½ cup egg substitute
   (2 eggs)
1 cup grated Cheddar cheese
1 can (5 oz) evaporated milk
1 cup baking mix
¼ cup water
slivered almonds (opt)

1. Pre-heat oven to 350 degrees.
2. Prepare and steam broccoli until crispy tender (or prepare broccoli according to package directions when using a purchased frozen product). Drain and set aside.
3. Melt margarine. Sauté onion, garlic, and mushrooms (opt) until tender.
4. Stir in seasonings. Add egg, cheese and milk.
5. Blend baking mix and water to form dough. Roll out and fit into a pie plate.
6. Pour broccoli mixture into the pastry shell.
7. Sprinkle slivered almonds on top for garnish (if desired). Bake 40–45 minutes.

Approx six servings
Per Servings

Calories	187	*Cholesterol*	4 mg
Protein	10 g	*Sodium*	329 mg
Carbohydrates	27 g	*Fat*	5 g

Calories from fat = 23%

NO FAIL BROCCOLI PIE

4 cups chopped broccoli
½ cup chopped onion
1 small green pepper,
  chopped
⅔ cup grated cheese
1½ cups milk

¾ cup baking mix
¾ cup egg substitute
  (3 eggs)
½ teas salt
other seasoning to taste

1. Preheat oven to 375 degrees. Grease a pie plate (preferably with non-stick vegetable spray).
2. Prepare and steam broccoli until crispy tender (or prepare broccoli according to the package directions when using a purchased frozen product). Drain.
3. Add onion, green pepper, and cheese. Pour into a pie plate.
4. Beat remaining ingredients together until smooth. Pour evenly over the broccoli.
5. Bake until golden brown (about 45–50 minutes), or until a knife or toothpick inserted comes out clean. Let stand 5 minutes before cutting.

Approx six servings
Per Serving

Calories	216	Cholesterol	7 mg
Protein	14 g	Sodium	347 mg
Carbohydrates	31 g	Fat	5 g

Calories from fat = 21%

MICROWAVE BROCCOLI QUICHE

1 lb. chopped broccoli
1 cup baking mix
¼ cup water
1½ Tbsp soy sauce
1 cup Mozzarella cheese

¾ cup egg substitute
 (3 eggs)
1 can (5 oz) evaporated milk
1 can French Fried onions
2 Tbsp chopped green onions

1. Prepare and steam broccoli until crispy tender (or prepare broccoli according to package directions when using a purchased frozen product). Drain and set aside.
2. Blend baking mix and water to form dough. Roll out and fit into a pie plate. Brush inside of pastry shell with soy sauce and prick with a fork.
3. Microwave on high for 4 minutes, rotating a half turn after two minutes.
4. Sprinkle cheese into crust. Spread broccoli evenly over the cheese.
5. Blend egg and evaporated milk together. Pour over the broccoli.
6. Cut through the canned onions with a knife, and sprinkle them over the pie mixture. Lightly press onions down. Top with chopped green onion.
7. Microwave on medium 11–13 minutes. Rotate a half turn after six minutes. Allow 5 minutes standing time to firm slightly before serving.

Approx six servings
Per Serving

Calories	298	Cholesterol	6 mg
Protein	19 g	Sodium	570 mg
Carbohydrates	42 g	Fat	8 g

Calories from fat = 24%

BROCCOLI CUSTARD

4 cups chopped broccoli
1½ cups milk
3 Tbsp flour
2 cups egg substitute
   (8 eggs)

¼ cup Parmesan cheese
paprika for garnish

1. Preheat oven to 350 degrees.
2. Prepare and steam broccoli until cripsy tender (or prepare broccoli according to package directions when using a purchased frozen product). Drain and set aside.
3. Blend milk, flour, salt and pepper together. Cook over low heat, stirring often, until thickened.
4. Pour egg into a bowl. Fold in grated cheese.
5. Add drained broccoli and milk sauce mixture to the eggs. Mix together.
6. Pour into a baking dish. Place in a larger pan, adding about 1" water in the larger pan. Bake for 65–75 minutes until custard is set.

Approx six servings
Per Serving

Calories	102	Cholesterol	6 mg
Protein	10 g	Sodium	161 mg
Carbohydrates	14 g	Fat	2 g

Calories from fat = 18%

BROCCOLI SOUFFLÉ

1 lb. chopped broccoli
1 cup Cheddar cheese
2 teas melted margarine
¾ cup egg substitute (3 eggs)
1 cup milk

½ teas salt
1 cup cut bread crumbs
  (¼" to ½ " cubes)
3 egg whites, stiffly beaten

1. Preheat oven to 350 degrees. Grease a baking dish (preferably with non-stick vegetable spray).
2. Prepare and steam broccoli until crispy tender (or prepare broccoli according to package directions when using a purchased frozen product). Drain then puree in blender.
3. Cut cheese into chunks and melt in microwave or in a double boiler.
4. Mix all the ingredients except the egg whites together. Blend until smooth.
5. Fold in the egg whites and place into a baking dish. Bake 1 hour. Soufflé is done when a knife or toothpick inserted comes out clean.

Approx six servings
Per Serving

Calories	179	*Cholesterol*	8 mg
Protein	17 g	*Sodium*	259 mg
Carbohydrates	22 g	*Fat*	4 g

Calories from fat = 20%

BROCCOLI RICE PILAF

1 Tbsp margarine
½ cup long grain rice,
  uncooked
¼ cup onion, chopped
½ cup celery, chopped
1 cup finely chopped broccoli

½ teas basil
salt & pepper to taste
1 env dry chicken noodle
  soup
1½ cups water

1. Melt margarine in a large pan. Add rice. Cook until browned, stirring frequently.
2. Add onion, celery, broccoli and seasonings. Sauté. Stir in spices, soup mix and water.
3. Cover and simmer 15 minutes. This recipe can easily be doubled.

Approx three servings
Per Serving

Calories	173	*Cholesterol*	0 mg
Protein	5 g	*Sodium*	274 mg
Carbohydrates	33 g	*Fat*	24 g

Calories from fat = 12%

GREEN RICE

2½ cups chopped broccoli
2 teas margarine
⅓ cup chopped onion
½ cup celery, chopped
1 can cream of chicken soup

½ cup milk
1 can (6 oz) water chestnuts
4 oz cheese, cut in chunks
1 small can mushrooms (opt)
3 cups cooked rice

1. Preheat oven to 350 degrees.
2. Prepare and steam broccoli until crispy tender (or prepare broccoli according to package directions when using a purchased frozen product). Drain and set aside.

3. Melt margarine in a saucepan. Sauté onion and celery. Add soup, milk, water chestnuts, cheese, and mushrooms (if desired). Mix and cook until cheese melts.
4. Mix in broccoli, salt and cooked rice. Pour into a baking dish. Bake 35 minutes.

Approx five servings
Per Serving

Calories	261	*Cholesterol*	13 mg
Protein	15 g	*Sodium*	343 mg
Carbohydrates	42 g	*Fat*	4 g

Calories from fat = 15%

BROCCOLI HODGEPODGE STEW

1 slice of bacon
1 small onion, chopped
1 potato, cut into ½" cubes
½ cup milk

salt and pepper to taste
other seasonings to taste
3 cups broccoli florets
2 carrots, sliced

1. Cook bacon in a small skillet until it begins to brown. Add onion, and cook on low heat until onion softens.
2. Add potato, ¼ cup milk, salt and pepper. Cook until the potato is nearly tender.
3. Add broccoli, carrots, and remaining milk. Cook until the vegetables are tender.
4. Thicken, if desired, with flour or cornstarch. Serve with biscuits or rolls.

Approx four servings
Per Serving

Calories	113	*Cholesterol*	3 mg
Protein	8 g	*Sodium*	81 mg
Carbohydrates	22 g	*Fat*	1 g

Calories from fat = 8%

BROCCOLI CHEESE RING

1 lb. broccoli spears
1 Bermuda onion, chopped
2 Tbsp margarine
2 Tbsp flour
salt & pepper

1½ cups milk
8 oz cheese, cut in chunks
¼ cup mayonnaise
12 slices toasted French
  bread

1. Trim broccoli, cut off bottom of stems, peel stems, then split lengthwise into spears. Steam 10–15 minutes until crispy tender. Drain and set aside.
2. Melt margarine and sauté onion until soft. Remove from heat.
3. Blend in flour, salt and pepper.
4. Gradually stir in milk. Cook over low heat, stirring constantly, until sauce thickens.
5. Stir in cheese and cook until melted. Fold in mayonnaise and blend well.
6. Arrange broccoli on a round plate with stems toward the middle.
7. Stand toast up between broccoli to form a circle then spoon sauce in the middle.

Approx six servings
Per Serving

Calories	397	*Cholesterol*	14 mg
Protein	25 g	*Sodium*	655 mg
Carbohydrates	54 g	*Fat*	9 g

Calories from fat = 19%

BROCCOLI 'N' DIP

Dip

broccoli broken into florets
other vegetables as desired

1 cup plain yogurt
1 pkg dry Ranch dressing
  mix

1. Blend yogurt and Ranch dressing mix together. Refrigerate until ready to serve.
2. Prepare vegetables as desired and arrange attractively on a tray for serving.

BROCCOLI VEGGIE PIZZA

2 pkg (8 count) Crescent rolls
1 pkg (8 oz) cream cheese, softened
1 cup sour cream
⅔ cup mayonnaise

1 envelope Ranch dressing
¾ cup each, chopped: broccoli, cauliflower, carrots, green pepper
¾ cup grated cheese

1. Preheat oven to 350 degrees.
2. Press the crescent rolls flat into an 11 × 13 pan. Bake 15 minutes, or until browned.
3. Blend cream cheese, sour cream, mayonnaise and Ranch dressing together then spread evenly over the cooled crust. (Option: To decrease calories/fat—instead of 1 cup sour cream, blend ¼ cup sour cream with ¾ cup tofu until smooth.)
4. Sprinkle vegetables and cheese evenly on top. Cover with plastic wrap. Press down.
5. Refrigerate 2 to 3 hours. Cut into squares. (Recipe can easily be cut in half.)

Approx eight servings
Per Serving

Calories	374	Cholesterol	37 mg
Protein	15 g	Sodium	637 mg
Carbohydrates	53 g	Fat	12 g

Calories from fat = 28%

BROCCOLI CROWN

1 lb. chopped broccoli
¼ cup onion, chopped
3 Tbsp margarine
2 Tbsp flour
½ teas salt
1½ cups milk

¾ cup egg substitute
  (3 eggs)
3 cups cooked rice
½ cup mayonnaise
½ teas marjoram
2 cups cherry tomatoes

1. Preheat oven to 350 degrees. Grease a ring mold (preferably with non-stick vegetable spray).
2. Prepare and steam broccoli until crispy tender (or prepare broccoli according to package directions when using a purchased frozen product). Drain and set aside.
3. Melt 1 Tbsp margarine in a small saucepan. Sauté onion until soft.
4. Stir in flour and salt. Gradually add milk. Cook, stirring constantly, until thickened.
5. Stir eggs into sauce. Continue cooking about 3 minutes until mixture thickens.
6. Remove from heat. Stir in rice, mayonnaise, and parsley (if desired).
7. Fold into drained broccoli then spoon into the ring mold.
8. Set ring mold pan inside a larger baking pan. Pour 1″ boiling water in outside pan.
9. Bake about 30 minutes, or until set. Remove from pan of water. Let stand several minutes then loosen around the edges with a knife and invert onto a serving plate.
10. Melt 2 Tbsp margarine. Add marjoram and tomatoes. Cook 5 minutes, just until heated through. Spoon herbed tomatoes into the center of the broccoli mold.

Approx six servings
Per Serving

Calories	231	Cholesterol	2 mg
Protein	10 g	Sodium	320 mg
Carbohydrates	42 g	Fat	4 g

Calories from fat = 14%

ELEPHANT BROCCOLI STEW

1 medium size elephant
1 ton of coarsely chopped
  broccoli

salt and pepper to taste
2 rabbits (opt)

1. Cut elephant into bite sized pieces . . . this will take about two months.
2. Add coarsely chopped broccoli and seasonings. Cover with water and cook in a very large kettle over an open fire for about four weeks.
3. If unexpected guests show up, two rabbits may be added, but only do this if necessary since nobody likes to fine "hare" in their stew!

Approximately 3500 servings